Management and Organizational Behavior

Compiled for: Professor Aimee Kane
Duquesne University
MGMT 261

Chapters Contributed From

Management Fundamentals, Ninth Edition,
by Robert N. Lussier

and

Group Dynamics for Teams, Fifth Edition,
by Daniel Levi

Los Angeles | London | New Delhi
Singapore | Washington DC | Melbourne

FOR INFORMATION:

SAGE Publications, Inc.
2455 Teller Road
Thousand Oaks, California 91320
E-mail: order@sagepub.com

SAGE Publications Ltd.
1 Oliver's Yard
55 City Road
London EC1Y 1SP
United Kingdom

SAGE Publications India Pvt. Ltd.
B 1/I 1 Mohan Cooperative Industrial Area
Mathura Road, New Delhi 110 044
India

SAGE Publications Asia-Pacific Pte. Ltd.
18 Cross Street #10-10/11/12
China Square Central
Singapore 048423

ISBN 978-1-0718-3201-1

Contents

Chapter 1. Management and Its History   1

From *Management Fundamentals, Ninth Edition*,
by Robert N. Lussier

Chapter 2. Strategic and Operational Planning   19

From *Management Fundamentals, Ninth Edition*,
by Robert N. Lussier

**Chapter 3. Communication, Information Technology,
and Emotional Intelligence**   59

From *Management Fundamentals, Ninth Edition*,
by Robert N. Lussier

Appendix A. Career Management and Networking   71

From *Management Fundamentals, Ninth Edition*,
by Robert N. Lussier

Appendix B. Guide to Student Team Projects   87

From *Group Dynamics for Teams, Fifth Edition*,
by Daniel Levi

1

Management and Its History

Learning Objectives

1-1. State how the study of management helps develop personal and professional skills. **PAGE 2**

1-2. Describe a manager's responsibility. **PAGE 3**

1-3. List the three skills of effective managers. **PAGE 5**

1-4. State the four management functions. **PAGE 8**

1-5. Explain the three management role categories. **PAGE 10**

1-6. Describe the differences among the hierarchy of management levels in terms of skills needed and functions performed. **PAGE 12**

1-7. Summarize the major similarities and differences between the classical and behavioral theorists. **PAGE 17**

Ideas on Management at JPMorgan Chase

Jamie Dimon is the CEO of **JPMorgan Chase**, a multinational investment bank and financial services firm based in New York City. It is the largest bank in the United States. The company operates under the guiding principles of client service, operational excellence, integrity, fairness and responsibility, and a winning culture.

Dimon is respected as a tough but fair leader who maintains high expectations for his followers but believes in supporting them by fostering a great corporate culture where associates can thrive. He also believes rewards and discipline should be linked to performance and that everyone needs to be held accountable for their actions.

Getty Images North America/Mark Wilson/Staff

$SAGE edge™

Get the edge on your studies: **edge.sagepub.com/lussier9e**

- Take a quiz to find out what you've learned.

- Review key terms with eFlashcards.

- Watch videos that enhance chapter content.

In recognition of his leadership ability, Dimon was listed as one of The World's 50 Greatest Leaders of 2019 by *Fortune* magazine.

> **IOM 1.** What resources does Jamie Dimon use in performing his job as CEO at JPMorgan Chase?
>
> **IOM 2.** Which qualities, skills, or competencies does Jamie Dimon use to be successful in his leadership role at JPMorgan Chase?
>
> **IOM 3.** How does Jamie Dimon execute management functions in his leadership role at JPMorgan Chase?
>
> **IOM 4.** Which management roles does Jamie Dimon play in performing his job as CEO at JPMorgan Chase?
>
> **IOM 5.** Which theories of management are reflected in Jamie Dimon's approach to leading JPMorgan Chase?

You'll find answers to these **IOM** questions throughout the chapter. To learn more about Dimon and JPMorgan Chase, visit jpmorganchase.com.

Sources: https://www.jpmorganchase.com/corporate/About-JPMC/ab-business-principles.htm; https://www.businessstudent.com/topics/12-things-all-business-students-can-learn-from-jamie-dimon/; http://fortune.com/worlds-greatest-leaders/. Accessed April 20, 2019.

Poll: Qualities of a Manager

In your opinion, which of the following is the most important quality of a successful manager?

- Enjoys working with people
- Motivates others
- Is a problem solver
- Is trustworthy
- Treats people fairly

Feedback: All of these qualities play a role in successful management. You can work on improving your skills in these areas throughout this course.

WHY STUDY MANAGEMENT?

>> **LO 1-1:** State how the study of management helps develop personal and professional skills.

It's natural at this point to think, "What can I get from this book?" or "What's in it for me?" Colleges are often criticized for a "relevance gap."[1] Do you want your college studies to prepare you for the workplace but question the relevance of your courses?[2] Do you want to develop skills you can use in your personal and professional life? The connection between the study of business management and its application in the workplace is the focus of this book. In this chapter, you will learn about the research-supported management skills and functions[3] that employers look for in all job recruits, and throughout the book you will be provided with opportunities to develop those skills. After you learn more about these skills and functions, we'll provide details for developing your skills in the "Objectives of the Book" section of this chapter.

Develop Skills You Can Use in Your Personal Life

Do you want to be happy? Well, true happiness comes from our relationships, not things.[4] Throughout this book, you can develop skills that can help you maintain and improve your personal relationships with family, friends, and coworkers. In just about every chapter, you can develop skills that can be used immediately in your personal lives. For example, in Skill Builder exercise 1-1 at the end of this chapter, you will learn a technique to help you remember people's names; in the next chapter you will find guides to ethical behavior; Chapter 4 presents a model that can help you make better decisions; Chapter 10 can improve your skills of resolving conflicts and managing your stress; and in Chapter 13 you can improve your communication skills.

Here is a tip for developing skills you can use in your personal life from **Sheryl Sandberg**, **Facebook** COO. If you want to be happier, have gratitude by focusing on the positive things in your life, not the negatives.[5] Gratitude is good for business.[6] Also, being happy is simple. Happiness arises from choosing to be happy, from not complaining and not dwelling on the negative things, and from being grateful for what you have and focusing on the positive things in your life.[7] This advice is based on research supporting the ideas that "If you can't be happy with what you have, then you can never be happy,"[8] and that gratitude improves life satisfaction.[9]

American society tends to promote two *isms* that tend to lead to personal unhappiness. The first is individualism—be selfish; look out for yourself; take advantage of others for your own personal gain, only do things that have something in them for you. The second is hedonism—don't do it if you don't feel like doing it; just do whatever makes you feel good.[10] Booker T. Washington said, "Those who are happiest are those who do the most for others."[11] Making sacrifices for others brings happiness.[12] Do you know any selfish people? Do you like them? Are they really happy? Will they ever be happy? Do you feel a sense of selfish entitled[13] with a lack of gratitude?[14] Are you happy? Are you content with the person you see in the mirror?[15] Through this book, you can develop your people skills and be happier.

Develop Skills You Can Use as a Manager or Employee

Let's extend happiness and success to our professional lives. **LinkedIn** cofounder **Reid Hoffman** says job satisfaction and success come from positive relationships at work.[16] Relationships formed at work are the core of our lives[17] and are reliable indicators of happiness for all ages.[18] Do workplace relationships bring you happiness?[19] Business success is based on developing and maintaining good relationships.[20] Former **Land O'Lakes** CEO **Jack Gherty** said he became successful and his company is doing so well because he focuses on helping other people win. **LinkAmerica** CEO **Andrés Ruzo** says the more you give, the more you get back.[21]

As management guru **Henry Mintzberg** said, "No job is more vital to our society than that of a manager."[22] Positive manager–subordinate relationships are invaluable to organizational success. If you are a manager or want to be a manager someday, you need good management skills to be successful,[23] and throughout this book, you will be given opportunities to develop your management skills.

But even if you are not interested in being a manager, you still need management skills to succeed in today's workplace. The old workplace, in which managers simply told employees what to do, is gone. Today, employees want to be involved in management, and organizations are recruiting employees with people skills who can work effectively in teams and share in decision-making and other management tasks.[24] At **Zappos**, they have even eliminated the term *manager* because they want employees to be self-managed.[25] Unfortunately, it has been said that new college graduates lack the ability to manage or lead.[26]

This book can help you develop management skills you can apply in your personal and professional life. In this chapter, you will learn what management is all about, and we will begin the discussion of how you can develop your management skills.

WHAT IS A MANAGER'S RESPONSIBILITY?

>> **LO 1-2:** Describe a manager's responsibility.

A **manager** is responsible for achieving organizational objectives through efficient and effective utilization of resources. *Efficient* means doing things right so as to maximize the utilization of resources. *Effective* means doing the right thing in order to

manager The individual responsible for achieving organizational objectives through efficient and effective utilization of resources.

manager's resources Human, financial, physical, and informational resources.

attain an objective. The manager's resources are human, financial, physical, and informational. How managers accumulate and allocate these resources affects both efficient and effective performance.[27] The resources are listed in Exhibit 1-1.

Human Resources

Human resources are people, often referred to as human capital.[28] **Wegmans** VP **Jack Depeters** says the success of any company depends on its employees.[29] In this way, people are an organization's most valuable assets, and this is especially true of its managers.[30] Throughout this book, we will focus on how managers work with employees to accomplish organizational objectives.

Financial Resources

It takes money to make money, and without proper finances, you don't have a business. Most managers have a budget stating the allocation of finances to operate their department or their store for a set period of time.[31] A major factor in the **Toys "R" Us** bankruptcy was financial mismanagement.[32]

Physical Resources

Managers are responsible for making the products and delivering services; keeping equipment in working condition; and ensuring that necessary products, materials, and supplies are available when needed. For example, **Amazon** stocks thousands of products in fulfillment centers around the world to provide fast delivery of its products.[33]

Informational Resources

You need information (including communication of information) to set objectives and make decisions on how to allocate and use your scarce resources to attain your objectives.[34] CEO **Richard Branson** of **Virgin Group** says information should flow freely throughout the organization to be used as a continuous learning process.[35] **Facebook** Chief Information Officer (CIO) **Timothy Campos** says his job is to use information technology (IT) to enable the efficiency and effectiveness of the company.[36]

Resources and Performance

performance Means of evaluating how effectively and efficiently managers utilize resources to achieve objectives.

Managers have a profound impact on the performance of their organizations.[37] So how you acquire and manage the four resources affects organizational performance.[38] The level of organizational performance *is based on how effectively and efficiently managers utilize resources to achieve objectives.* Managers are responsible for setting and evaluating how well they meet organizational strategies and objectives through utilization and control of resources.[39] Selecting the right resources—being effective—and using them efficiently results in creativity and high levels of performance.[40]

Jamie Dimon (IOM 1) believes strongly in the importance of human resources which involves the acquisition and development of the very best talent in terms of intelligence, analytical skills, and work ethic. He maintains high standards for his employees, but believes in rewarding them for good performance as well. Dimon also uses informational resources effectively. He believes in maintaining a strong emphasis on getting the most critical information and analyzing and processing it in the most efficient manner possible.

EXHIBIT 1-1

Management Resources

| Human |
| Financial |
| Physical |
| Informational |

WORK APPLICATION 1-1

Describe specific examples of the four resources used by a present or past boss. Give the manager's job title and department.

A Manager Interview

This interview with **Bonnie Castonguary**, a store manager for **Gap Inc.**, provides an overview of the manager's job and responsibility.

Q: What was your progression to your present job as store manager?

A: I started as a store manager in training. I replaced a woman on maternity leave as acting store manager, and then I had my first store. After a while, I was promoted to larger stores with more sales volume. A few years later, I was promoted to manager of [a] Gap outlet store.... My next career advancement is to general manager.... I would still be in one store, but I would assist the district manager by overseeing other stores in my district.

Q: Briefly describe your job.

A: Gap Inc.'s two-page "Position Overview Store Management" form, which also contains a detailed summary for each level of management, presents this general summary: "The Store Management team manages the sales, operations, and personnel functions of the store to ensure maximum profitability and compliance with company procedures. The Team includes Assistant Managers, Associate Managers, the Store Manager, and/or the General Manager."

Q: What do you like best about being a manager?

A: You don't have time to get bored on the job because you are always doing something different.

Q: What do you like least about being a manager?

A: Dealing with difficult performance problems of employees and customers, and always being on call. When I'm not at work, I'm still on call when there are problems at the store. This could mean going to the store at 2:00 a.m. to shut off the alarm.

Q: What advice would you give to college graduates without any full-time work experience who are interested in a management career after graduation?

A: You need to be dedicated and hardworking. You must take great pride in your work. You have to be willing to take on a lot of responsibility. Remember, your employees are always looking to you to set the example; when you make a mistake (which you will do), it affects your staff. You have to be a self-starter. As a store manager, you have to motivate employees, but your boss is not around much to motivate you.

WHAT DOES IT TAKE TO BE A SUCCESSFUL MANAGER?

>> **LO 1-3:**   **List the three skills of effective managers.**

Although managers' jobs vary, researchers generally agree on a set of qualities, skills, and competencies necessary to be a successful manager.

Management Qualities

"What does it take to be a successful manager?" "What are the most important traits for success as a supervisor?" Before you read about these traits. Complete Self-Assessment 1-1 on management traits to find out if you have these qualities. Self-awareness[41] and self-assessment[42] are the crucial first step for improvement. You will have the opportunity to complete self-assessments in every chapter to help you identify skills to improve in your personal and professional lives.

Integrity, industriousness, and the ability to get along with people have been identified as the three most important traits for successful managers.[43]

1-1 SELF-ASSESSMENT

Management Traits

The following 15 questions relate to some of the qualities needed to be a successful manager. Rate yourself on each item by indicating with a number (1–4) how well each statement describes you.

1. The statement does not describe me at all.

2. The statement somewhat describes me.

3. The statement describes me most of the time.

4. The statement describes me very accurately.

_____ 1. I enjoy working with people. I prefer to work with others rather than working alone.

_____ 2. I can motivate others. I can get people to do things they may not want to do.

_____ 3. I am well liked. People enjoy working with me.

_____ 4. I am cooperative. I strive to help the team do well rather than to be the star.

_____ 5. I am a leader. I enjoy teaching, coaching, and instructing people.

_____ 6. I want to be successful. I do things to the best of my ability to be successful.

_____ 7. I am a self-starter. I get things done without having to be told to do them.

_____ 8. I am a problem solver. If things aren't going the way I want them to, I take corrective action to meet my objectives.

_____ 9. I am self-reliant. I don't need the help of others.

_____ 10. I am hardworking. I enjoy working and getting the job done.

_____ 11. I am trustworthy. If I say I will do something by a set time, I do it.

_____ 12. I am loyal. I do not do or say things to intentionally hurt my friends, relatives, or coworkers.

_____ 13. I can take criticism. If people tell me negative things about myself, I give them serious thought and change when appropriate.

_____ 14. I am honest. I do not lie, steal, or cheat.

_____ 15. I am fair. I treat people equally. I don't take advantage of others.

_____ TOTAL SCORE (add numbers on lines 1–15; the range of possible scores is 15–60)

In general, the higher your score, the better your chances of being a successful manager. You can work on improving your *integrity* (items 11–15), *industriousness* (items 6–10), and ability to get along with *people* (items 1–5) both in this course and in your personal life. As a start, review the traits listed here. Which ones are your strongest and weakest? Think about how you can improve in the weaker areas—or, even better, write out a plan.

Management Skills

management skills The skills needed to be an effective manager, including technical, interpersonal, and decision-making skills.

Skills involve the ability to perform some type of activity or task. **Management skills** *include (1) technical, (2) interpersonal, and (3) decision-making skills.* Technical skills can be referred to as hard skills, whereas interpersonal and decision-making skills are often called soft skills, and the most sought-after skills in the job market are soft skills because organizations seek employees at all levels and positions (including technology jobs) who can communicate clearly, problem solve and get along with coworkers.[44] Because management skills are so important, the focus of this book is on skill building. If you work at it, you can develop your management skills through this course.

Technical Skills

technical skills The ability to use methods and techniques to perform a task.

Technical skills *involve the ability to use methods and techniques to perform a task.* All employees need technical skills to perform their jobs. A manager may develop a budget (managerial job) using **Microsoft** Excel (technical skill). Technical skills are more important for employees than for managers, and they vary widely from job to job; therefore, this course does not focus on developing these skills. Although technology is advancing, it is people with interpersonal skills working effectively in teams who develop the technology.[45]

Interpersonal Skills

Interpersonal skills *involve the ability to understand, communicate with, and work well with individuals and groups through developing effective relationships.* Interpersonal skills are sometimes also referred to as human or people skills, as well as soft skills. Our relationships and happiness are based on our interpersonal skills.[46] They include the ability to communicate, motivate, and lead.[47]

> **interpersonal skills** The ability to understand, communicate with, and work well with individuals and groups through developing effective relationships.

If having good human relations are not very important, then why doesn't everyone at work get along, why do companies seek employees with good people skills,[48] and why are companies spending millions to develop employees' interpersonal skills? The resources you need to get the job done are made available through relationships.[49] Sir **Richard Branson** says, "You definitely need to be good with people to help bring out the best in people."[50] Several chapters focus on developing your interpersonal skills, especially the leadership section (Chapters 10–13).

Decision-Making Skills

Clearly, the decisions you have made over your lifetime have affected you today. Organizations are seeking employees with conceptual critical thinking skills that can take initiative to solve problems.[51] Leadership decisions determine the success or failure of organizations,[52] so organizations are also training their people to improve their decision-making skills. **Decision-making skills** *are based on the ability to conceptualize situations and select alternatives to solve problems and take advantage of opportunities.* You will develop your decision-making skills in Chapter 4.

> **decision-making skills** The ability to conceptualize situations and select alternatives to solve problems and take advantage of opportunities.

Jamie Dimon (IOM 2) clearly possesses the three type of management skills: technical, interpersonal, and decision making. He is known in the financial services industry as a leading thinker. He possesses superior analytical and strategic skills that support the achievement of his business objectives at **JPMorgan Chase**. Dimon is known as a demanding leader, but he demonstrates interpersonal skills in his belief in encouraging his executives to balance work and play and his practice of rewarding loyalty from his followers. Dimon uses his decision-making skills to literally make hundreds of strategic and operational decisions on a daily basis associated with running a leading financial services company. His decisions shape the direction and future success of his company.

To summarize, technical skills are primarily concerned with things, interpersonal skills are primarily concerned with people, and decision-making skills are primarily concerned with ideas and concepts. Review the management skills in Exhibit 1-2; then complete Applying the Concept 1-1.

EXHIBIT 1-2

Management Skills

Technical Skills
Interpersonal Skills
Decision-Making Skills

AACSB Competencies

In addition to qualities and skills, the **AACSB International (Association to Advance Collegiate Schools of Business)** has established standards for accreditation of business schools; they were updated effective January 1, 2019. The standards curricula address general content areas—skills and knowledge and encourage active student engagement.

General Skill Areas to be developed include (identifies chapters developing this knowledge and skill): Written and oral communication (Ch 13), Ethical understanding and reasoning (Ch 2), Analytical thinking (all), Information technology (Ch 13), Interpersonal relations and teamwork (Ch 8), Diverse and multicultural work environments (Ch 3), Reflective thinking (all), Application of knowledge (all), Integration of real-world business experiences (your personal use of the skills).[53]

This book includes Applications and Skill Builders at the end of each chapter to foster the development of your management qualities, skills, and competencies. Each exercise identifies the AACSB General Skill area of development.

1-1 APPLYING THE CONCEPT

Management Skills

Identify each activity as being one of the following types of management skills:

A. technical

B. interpersonal

C. decision making

_____ 1. The manager is in a meeting making a presentation.

_____ 2. The manager is working on fixing a broken machine.

_____ 3. The manager is sending an email letting the employees know they exceeded the sales goal.

_____ 4. The manager is scheduling which machines will produce each product next week.

_____ 5. The manager is trying to figure out a way to solve a problem.

_____ 6. The manager is giving an employee praise for a job well done.

EXHIBIT 1-3

Management Functions

Planning
Organizing
Leading
Controlling

In addition to AACSB, this book also meets the core professional components of **ACBSP (Accreditation Council for Business Schools and Programs)**,[54] and **IACBE (International Assembly for Collegiate Business Education)** standards.[55] AACSB, ACBSP, and IACBE standards can be classified within the three management skills areas.[56]

MANAGEMENT FUNCTIONS

>> **LO 1-4:**   **State the four management functions.**

Years of research have shown that essentially everything a manager does can be classified into one of the four management functions or as nonmanagerial work. Performing the management functions clearly is difficult real work, and managers may also perform employee tasks.

The four **management functions** are *planning, organizing, leading,* and *controlling.* Managers perform the management functions through using organizational resources to achieve organizational objectives through others,[57] often in teams.[58] All of the Skill Builder exercises identify the management function skill being developed through the activity. Exhibit 1-3 lists the four functions of management.

management functions
Planning, organizing, leading, and controlling.

Planning—Based on Objectives

planning The process of setting objectives and determining in advance exactly how the objectives will be met.

Planning is typically the starting point in the management process, and you should begin with a clear objective.[59] **Planning** *is the process of setting objectives and determining in advance exactly how the objectives will be met.* There is a relationship between planning and performance.[60] So before we do anything, we should have an objective stating the end result and then develop a plan for how to complete it. You should also realize the other three functions also focus on achieving your objectives. You will learn how to write effective objectives and plans in Part II: Planning (Chapters 4–6).

Organizing

organizing The process of delegating and coordinating tasks and allocating resources to achieve objectives.

Performance is based on how managers organize their resources within the strategic process.[61] **Organizing** *is the process of delegating and coordinating tasks and allocating resources to achieve objectives.* An important part of coordinating human resources is to assign people to various jobs and tasks. So we design our work to achieve our objectives. An important part of organizing, sometimes listed as a separate function, is staffing. *Staffing* is the process of selecting, training, and evaluating employees.[62] You will learn how to organize in Part III: Organizing (Chapters 7–9).

Leading

The ability to lead is an important skill for everyone, especially for managers, because leadership contributes to organizational success.[63] A survey found that 63% of companies screen new hires on the basis of leadership ability.[64] **Leading** *is the process of influencing employees to work toward achieving objectives.* Managers must communicate the objectives to employees and motivate them to achieve those objectives by developing positive relationships.[65] You will learn how to lead in Part IV: Leading (Chapters 10–13).

leading The process of influencing employees to work toward achieving objectives.

Controlling

Objectives to achieve anything will not be met without consistent monitoring and measuring of your progress towards meeting the objectives, as well as overcoming obstacles to accomplish the objective. **Controlling** *is the process of monitoring and measuring progress and taking corrective action when needed to ensure that objectives are achieved.* You will learn how to control in Part V: Controlling (Chapters 14–15).

controlling The process of monitoring progress and taking corrective action when needed to ensure that objectives are achieved.

WORK APPLICATION 1-3

Identify a specific manager, preferably one who is or was your manager, and give examples of how that person performs each of the four management functions.

Nonmanagement Functions

All managers perform the four functions of management as they get work done through employees. However, many managers perform nonmanagement, or employee, functions as well. For example, at **Taco Bell** and **Chick-fil-A** it is common for store managers to cook or wait on customers at mealtimes, which is a nonmanagement function. Many managers are called working managers because they perform both management and employee functions.

Jamie Dimon (IOM 3) needs to address all of the management functions to be an effective leader. His long-term vision for **JPMorgan Chase** and the initiatives he helps to create require a superior planning process. He also needs to create an organizational structure that will, as he says, "institutionalize" best practices for getting things done and achieving desired business results. Dimon effectively leads JPMorgan Chase by fostering a corporate culture that supports the firm's strategy and maintaining high performance standards for his followers. Finally, he uses controlling to ensure the successful achievement of the firm's goals and strategies by rewarding exceptional performance and disciplining poor performance.

The Transition to Management—Managing People

Going from being an employee to being a manager is not an easy transition.[66] New managers often don't realize just how hard the job really is and how much more work managers do than employees, who constantly interrupt them, putting demands on their time. Because most new managers are used to doing nonmanagement functions, they often do the work for employees when their actual job is to train employees to do their job, help them improve their performance, and solve problems to make their jobs easier and less frustrating.

A current term for the transition is *"go suit,"* defined as getting promoted to management—and forgetting your basic job skills once installed in an office.[67] This is because as a manager, you get the job done through employees, or your job is to manage people—using interpersonal skills.[68] As a new manager, you will likely need to perform nonmanagement functions, but be sure to focus on planning, organizing, leading, and controlling to get the job done through people.

Management Functions

Indicate which type of function the manager is performing in each situation:

A. planning

B. organizing

C. leading

D. controlling

E. nonmanagement

_____ 7. The manager is encouraging an employee to get a college degree so she can become a manager.

_____ 8. The manager is conducting a job interview to select a new employee for a new open position in sales.

_____ 9. The manager is emptying his trash.

_____ 10. The manager is scheduling employee work hours for next week.

_____ 11. The manager is giving the workers a pep talk to motivate them to work hard to meet the production quota today with an absent employee.

_____ 12. The manager is conducting an employee's annual performance evaluation.

_____ 13. The manager is checking how many new computers have been produced so far today.

_____ 14. The manager is greeting customers as they enter the retail store asking if she can be of assistance finding anything.

MANAGEMENT ROLES

>> **LO 1.5:** **Explain the three management role categories.**

Managers have a set of distinct roles. A *role* is a set of expectations of how one will behave in a given situation. **Henry Mintzberg** identified 10 roles that managers play as they accomplish management functions. Mintzberg grouped these 10 roles into three **management role categories:**[69] *interpersonal, informational, and decisional roles* (see Exhibit 1-4).

management role categories
The categories of roles—interpersonal, informational, and decisional—managers play as they accomplish management functions.

Interpersonal Roles

When managers play interpersonal roles, they use their interpersonal skills as they perform management functions. Managers play the *figurehead* role when they represent the organization or department in ceremonial and symbolic activities. Managers play the *leader* role when they motivate, train, communicate with, and influence others. Managers play the *liaison* role when they interact with people outside of their unit to gain information and favors.

Informational Roles

When managers play informational roles, they use their interpersonal skills. Managers play the *monitor* role when they read and talk to others to receive information. Managers play the *disseminator* role when they send information to others. Managers play the *spokesperson* role when they provide information to people outside the organization.

Decisional Roles

When managers play decisional roles, they use their conceptual decision-making management skills. Managers play the *entrepreneur* role when they innovate and initiate improvements. Managers play the *disturbance-handler* role when they take corrective

EXHIBIT 1-4

Management Roles

MANAGEMENT ROLE CATEGORIES	MANAGEMENT ROLES WITHIN THE CATEGORY
Interpersonal	Figurehead, Leader, Liaison
Informational	Monitor, Disseminator, Spokesperson
Decisional	Entrepreneur, Disturbance handler, Resource allocator, Negotiator

action during disputes or crisis situations. Managers play the *resource-allocator* role when they schedule, request authorization, and perform budgeting and programming activities, as when managers perform the *negotiator* role when they represent their department or organization during nonroutine transactions to gain agreement and commitment.

Jamie Dimon (IOM 4) needs to wear many "hats" or take on many roles in performing his job. For example, he plays the liaison interpersonal role as he is the face of **JPMorgan Chase** and is responsible for managing relationships with external stakeholders such as customers, investors, government and industry leaders, etc. This is related to the spokesperson informational role as Dimon represents the company when making major announcements to the public and other stakeholder groups. In terms of decisional roles, Dimon is a resource allocator as he decides how the firm's financial and human resources will be directed to reflect the strategic priorities and business objectives of the overall company.

WORK APPLICATION 1-4

Identify a specific manager, preferably one who is or was your boss, and give examples of how that person performs roles in each of the three management role categories. Be sure to identify at least one of the three or four roles in each category.

The Systems Relationship Among the Management Skills, Functions, and Roles

It is important to understand system interrelationships.[70] The management skills are interrelated, or have a systems effect.[71] For example, a first-line supervisor's technical skills will affect his or her interpersonal and decision-making skills and vice versa. A manager's skills also affect the implementation of the management functions and roles.

The management functions are not steps in a linear process. Managers do not usually plan, then organize, then lead, and then control. The functions are distinct yet interrelated. Managers often perform them simultaneously. In addition, each function depends on the others. For example, if you start with a poor plan, the objective will not be met even if things are well organized, led, and controlled. Or if you start with a

---

1-3 APPLYING THE CONCEPT

Management Roles

Identify each of the managerial activities as part of one of the three role categories and its role within each category:

A. interpersonal role (1 Figurehead, 2 Leader, 3 Liaison)

B. informational role (1 Monitor, 2 Disseminator, 3 Spokesperson)

C. decisional role (1 Entrepreneur, 2 Disturbance handler, 3 Resource allocator, 4 Negotiator)

_____ _____ 15. The manager is meeting with two employees to resolve a conflict between them.

_____ _____ 16. The sales manager is meeting with the production manager about a customer order.

_____ _____ 17. The manager is sending an email with the new work schedule to employees for next week.

_____ _____ 18. The manager discusses next year's budget.

_____ _____ 19. The mayor is cutting the ribbon at the groundbreaking for the new town hall.

_____ _____ 20. The manager develops a new app that will be sold as an additional source of income.

_____ _____ 21. The manager is reading the monthly budget report.

_____ _____ 22. The manager shows a new employee how to record her working hours.

EXHIBIT 1-5

Management Skills, Functions, and Roles

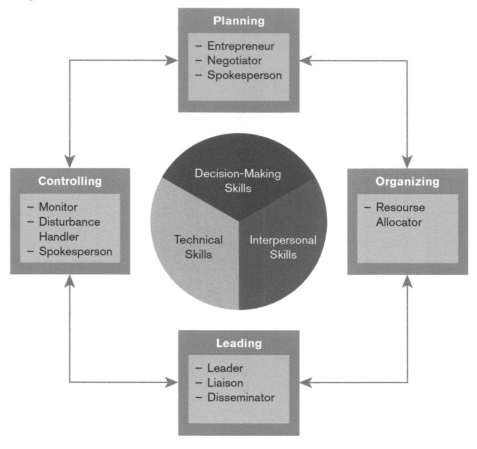

great plan but are poorly organized or lead poorly, the objective may not be met. Plans without controls are rarely implemented effectively. Remember that the management functions are based on setting objectives (planning) and achieving them (through organizing, leading, and controlling).

How well a manager plays the various management roles is also affected by his or her management skills. The 10 management roles are also integrated with the management functions. Certain management roles are played when performing the different management functions.

Exhibit 1-5 illustrates the interrelationship of *management skills, functions,* and *roles.*

DIFFERENCES AMONG MANAGERS

>> LO 1-6:   **Describe the differences among the hierarchy of management levels in terms of skills needed and functions performed.**

As you will learn in this section, there are different levels of managers, and the importance of the skills and functions needed to perform the job varies by level. We will also discuss some of the differences between business sizes and managing for-profit companies and not-for-profit organizations.

The Three Levels of Management

Managers differ in the level of management, and there are also nonpermanent managers called team leaders, as well as nonmanager operative employees. There are also different types of managers by level of management. Let's cover these concepts in this sequence.

The three **levels of management** are *top managers, middle managers, and first-line managers*. Job titles are given to help identify the level of management.[72] The three levels relate to each other as described here. See Exhibit 1-6 for an illustration of the three levels of management and operative employees.

levels of management Top managers, middle managers, and first-line managers.

Top Management

Top managers—people in executive positions—have titles such as CEO, president, or vice president. Most organizations have relatively few top management positions. Top managers are responsible for managing an entire organization or major parts of it. They develop and define the organization's purpose, objectives, and strategies. They report to boards of directors or other executives and supervise the activities of middle managers.

Middle Management

People in middle-manager positions have titles such as marketing and operations manager, and department head. Middle managers are responsible for implementing top management's strategy by developing short-term operating plans. They generally report to executives and supervise the work of first-line managers.

Large corporations have multiple levels of management that serve different purposes to the organization. Levi Strauss's CEO Chip Bergh **is a top manager who steered the company back to its position of prominence in American culture.**

©iStockphoto.com/Akespyker

First-Line Management

Examples of titles of first-line managers are sales and accounting supervisor, and office manager. These managers are responsible for implementing middle managers'

Management Levels and Functional Areas

Top Management

President

Middle Management

Marketing manager	Operations manager	Finance manager	Human resources manager

First-Line Management

Advertising supervisor	Sales supervisor	Product A supervisor	Product B supervisor	Accounting supervisor	Finance supervisor	Benefits supervisor	Training supervisor

Nonmanagers—Operative Employees

Operatives	Operatives	Operatives	Operatives	Operatives	Operatives	Operatives	Operatives

operational plans. They generally report to middle managers. Unlike those at the other two levels of management, first-line managers do not supervise other managers; they supervise operative employees (nonmanagers).

WORK APPLICATION 1-5

Identify the levels of management in a specific organization by level and title. Be sure to give the organization's name.

Team Leader

This is a newer management position needed in organizations that focus on a team-based structure. They can have a significant impact on performance.[73] They are often called a project or program leader or task force or committee leader. The team leader facilitates team activities to achieve a goal rather than telling people what to do.

Higher-level managers may also be team leaders who supervise a small group of people to achieve a goal. Nonmanagement operative employees may also be team leaders who manage a team until the goal is completed. The team leader is not usually a permanent management position and thus is not a level in the hierarchy of management. You will learn more about teams and how to lead them in Chapter 8.

Nonmanagement Operative Employees

Operative employees are the workers in an organization who do not hold management positions. They commonly report to first-line managers and possibly to team leaders. They make the products, wait on customers, perform repairs, and so on.

Types of Managers by Level

types of managers General managers, functional managers, and project managers.

The three **types of managers** are general managers, functional managers, and project managers. Top-level and some middle managers are general managers because they supervise the activities of several departments that perform different activities. Middle and first-line managers are often business functional managers who supervise the completion of related tasks. Project managers are often team leaders.

The four most common *business functional* areas include marketing (sell the products and services), operations/production (make the product or perform the service), finance/accounting (maintain financial records), and human resources/personnel management (hire and compensate employees), as shown in Exhibit 1-6. We will discuss these functional areas in Chapter 7.

A project manager coordinates employees and other resources across several functional departments to accomplish a specific goal or task, such as developing a new aircraft at **Boeing**.

Differences in Management Skills

All managers need technical, interpersonal, and decision-making skills. However, the relative importance of these types of skills varies with the level of management. At all three levels of management, the need for interpersonal skills remains fairly constant. However, top-level managers have a greater need for decision-making skills, whereas first-line managers have a greater need for technical skills. Middle managers tend to need all three skills, but the mix required differs somewhat from organization to organization.

Differences in Management Functions

All managers perform the four management functions: planning, organizing, leading, and controlling. However, the time spent on each function varies with the level of management. First-line managers spend more time leading and controlling, middle-level managers spend equal time on all four functions, and top managers spend more time planning and organizing.

 Executive Compensation

In 2018, the AFL-CIO Paywatch reported CEOs of S&P 500 Index companies received an average of $13.94 million in total compensation. **Broadcom** CEO **Hock Tan** was the highest payed with $103.2 million, while **Alphabet (Google** cofounder) CEO **Larry Page** paid himself just $1. In contrast, production and nonsupervisory workers earned only an average of $38,613—a CEO-to-worker pay ratio of 361 to 1.

Some say top executives are being overpaid. In one of the largest corporate paydays in history, Chinese smartphone maker **Xiaomi** gave its CEO **Lei Jun** $1.5 billion in stock with no strings attached. Especially because some of the best-performing CEOs aren't the highest paid, including the best returns by **Nektar** CEO **Howard Robin.** Other CEOs get large raises even when the companies lose money. **Under Armour** CEO **Kevin Plank** had the worst results as the company return dropped by just over 50%.

However, not everyone agrees that top executives are overpaid. In capitalist countries, talented CEOs, like athletes in pro sports, are entitled to fetch their price, as most compensation is geared toward results. Top executives should be paid multimillion-dollar compensation packages; after all, if it weren't for effective CEOs, companies would not be making the millions of dollars of profits they make each year. CEOs deserve a piece of the pie they helped bake.

1. Do executives deserve to make 361 times more than the average worker?

2. Is it ethical for managers to take large pay increases when laying off employees?

3. Is it ethical for managers to get pay raises when their companies lose money?

4. Are companies being socially responsible when paying executives premium compensation?

Sources: Information taken from the AFL-CIO's website at https://aflcio.org/paywatch, accessed February 26, 2019; MyLogIQ information reported in *The Wall Street Journal* (May 10, 2018): B1; J. Steinberg, "Xiaomi Gives Its CEO $1.5 Billion Thank You," *The Wall Street Journal* (June 23–24, 2018): A1, A7.

Differences Among Management Levels

Identify the level of management in the following five instances:

A. top

B. middle

C. first-line

_____ 23. Managers who report to executives.

_____ 24. Managers who need technical skills more than decision-making skills.

_____ 25. Managers who tend to spend more time planning and organizing.

_____ 26. Managers who have operative employees reporting to them.

_____ 27. Managers who take the long-term strategy and develop short-term operating plans.

EXHIBIT 1-7

Skills Needed and Functions Performed at Different Management Levels

MANAGEMENT LEVEL	PRIMARY MANAGEMENT SKILLS NEEDED	PRIMARY MANAGEMENT FUNCTIONS PERFORMED
Top	Decision-Making and Interpersonal Skills	Planning and Organizing
Middle	Balance of All Three	Balance of All Four
First-Line	Technical and Interpersonal Skills	Leading and Controlling

EXHIBIT 1-8

Differences Between Large and Small Businesses

FUNCTIONS AND ROLES	LARGE BUSINESS	SMALL BUSINESS
Planning	Commonly have formal written objectives and plans with a global business focus.	Commonly have informal objectives and plans that are not written with a global focus.
Organizing	Tend to have formal organization structures with clear policies and procedures, with three levels of management. Jobs tend to be specialized.	Tend to have informal structures without clear policies and procedures, with fewer than three levels of management. Jobs tend to be more general.
Leading	Managers tend to be more participative, giving employees more say in how they do their work and allowing them to make more decisions.	Entrepreneurs tend to be more autocratic and want things done their way, often wanting to make the decisions.
Controlling	Tend to have more sophisticated computerized control systems.	Tend to use less sophisticated control systems and to rely more on direct observation.
Important management roles	Resource allocator	Entrepreneur and spokesperson

Exhibit 1-7 (previous page) summarizes the primary skills needed and functions performed at each of the three management levels.

Differences in Size

Managers in large and small firms need the same skills and perform the same functions. However, generally, the larger the company, the more specialized the job. **Bonnie Castonguary** works for a large organization—**Gap Inc.** Her independent store resembles a small business, but it has the support of a large organization. More than 90 percent of all companies globally are small businesses, so they are important to economic growth,[74] even though they tend to have fewer resources. Exhibit 1-8 lists some of the differences between large and small businesses. However, these are general statements; many large and small businesses share certain characteristics. Most large businesses, including **Amazon**, **Apple**, and **Twitter**, started as small businesses and grew.

WORK APPLICATION 1-6

Would you prefer to work for a small or large business and a for-profit or not-for-profit organization?

Differences in Profits

Is the manager's job the same in for-profit and not-for-profit organizations? Although some noteworthy differences exist (volunteers and fundraising), the answer is basically yes. All managers need management skills, perform management functions, and play management roles regardless of the organization type. **Bonnie Castonguary** works for a for-profit business, **Gap Inc.** Employees of the **American Red Cross, Caffe Lena,** and the **YMCA** work for the public (not-for-profit) sector. Is the college you are attending for profit or not?

In the past, it was common to classify both nongovernmental and governmental organizations together into one group called not-for-profits. However, the current trend with globalization is to distinguish not-for-profit organizations into nongovernmental organizations (NGOs), such as **Doctors Without Borders** and governmental organizations, such as the Internal Revenue Service.

Exhibit 1-9 lists some of the differences between for-profit and not-for-profit organizations. You may not realize it, but there are more than 140 million volunteers across

EXHIBIT 1-9

Survey Results Comparing Large and Small Businesses' Responses

STATEMENT	SMALL BUSINESS RESPONSE PERCENTAGE*	LARGE BUSINESS RESPONSE PERCENTAGE*
My immediate manager is flexible when I need to take care of a personal or family matter.	91%	81%
The company supports me in achieving a reasonable balance between work and my personal life.	65%	60%
I believe the company will be successful over the next two to three years.	63%	72%
I have trust and confidence in the company's senior leadership team.	56%	63%
I believe my salary is fair, considering the pay of people doing similar work in other companies.	35%	49%
I plan to continue working for the company for more than five years.	36%	59%

* Percentage of employees who agreed with the statements
Source: Adapted from Korn Ferry's Hay Group Survey, Reported in *INC.* (November 2016), p. 44.

37 countries that play a critical role in a functioning society, as they contribute around $400 billion to the global economy annually.[75]

Redacted in this page

5

Strategic and Operational Planning

Learning Objectives

After studying this chapter, you should be able to:

5-1. Describe how strategic planning differs from operational planning. **PAGE 148**

5-2. Explain the reason for conducting an industry, competitive, and company situation analysis. **PAGE 151**

5-3. State the criteria for an effectively written objective by identifying must and want criteria. **PAGE 156**

5-4. Discuss corporate-level strategies in terms of the four grand strategies and the three growth strategies. **PAGE 159**

5-5. Summarize the three business-level adaptive and competitive strategies. **PAGE 164**

5-6. Identify strategies for short-range operational planning. **PAGE 166**

5-7. Describe the value of a time log analysis. **PAGE 170**

5-8. Explain the importance of implementing and controlling strategies. **PAGE 175**

Ideas on Management at the Ultimate Fighting Championship (UFC)

The **Ultimate Fighting Championship (UFC)** was started by **Rorion Gracie** and **Art Davie** in 1993 as an eight-man tournament where fighters with backgrounds in various martial arts such as Brazilian jiu jitsu, Muay Thai boxing, karate, boxing, kickboxing, and so on, competed to determine the superior fighter, with no rules governing the fight.

In 2000, **Station Casinos** executives **Frank** and **Lorenzo Fertitta**, along with their business partner **Dana White**, reached a deal to purchase the UFC with **Zuffa, LLC**, becoming the parent company. Under White's leadership, the UFC started to grow in popularity due to increased advertising, corporate sponsorships, and pay-per-view options for customers. Gradually, UFC events were held in high profile venues in Las Vegas such as the MGM Grand, and Fox Sports Net and the *Best Damn Sports Show Period* broadcasted tournaments over cable television. A reality TV show, *Ultimate Fighter*, was developed as a way to promote the UFC, and it was an instant success. This was followed by another show called *UFC*

Photo by Jeff Bottari/Zuffa LLC/Zuffa LLC via Getty Images

Unleashed. The key to the growth in popularity of the UFC was pay-per-view revenue for matches.

In 2017, the UFC reported record profits of over $700 million, and its popularity appears to be continuing to grow around the world.

- **IOM 1.** What is the mission of the UFC? Do you think it is an effective mission? Why or why not?

- **IOM 2.** What are the environmental factors that the UFC needs to consider in relation to its planning processes?

- **IOM 3.** What is the UFC's competitive advantage? Do you think that it is sustainable?

- **IOM 4.** What type of corporate strategies are being implemented by the UFC?

- **IOM 5.** What types of operational plans are being implemented by the UFC? Are the operational plans aligned with the corporate strategies?

Sources: https://www.forbes.com/sites/paulgift/2017/12/29/looking-ahead-2018-should-be-a-big-year-for-ufc-business-story-lines/#2b028bb442e0; https://www.mmawild.com/ufc/; https://www.eventmarketer.com/article/how-the-ufc-evolved-into-one-of-the-worlds-fastest-growing-sports-properties/; http://mikhail2012ufc.blogspot.com/2012/09/chapter-2-strategic-planning-for.html; http://mikhail2012ufc.blogspot.com/2012/09/chapter-1-mission-statement.html; https://www.bevnet.com/news/2018/body-armor-heads-ufc-octagon-official-sports-drink.

Poll: Time Management

How often do distractions and interruptions stop you from doing more important work?

- – Frequently (more than 10 times per day)

- – Occasionally (between 5 and 10 times per day)

- – Seldom (fewer than 5 times per day)

- – Never

Feedback: Our biggest time waster is often unnecessary interruptions. We need blocks of uninterrupted time without distractions to be productive. You will learn techniques and strategies for managing your time in this chapter.

STRATEGIC AND OPERATIONAL PLANNING

>> **LO 5-1:**   **Describe how strategic planning differs from operational planning.**

Recall from Chapter 1 that planning is the process of setting objectives and determining in advance exactly how the objectives will be met, and from the last chapter that decisions need plans for their implementation.[1] So before we take action, we need to set an objective and develop a plan. There is an old saying: "When you fail to plan, you plan to fail." Some managers complain that they don't have time to plan, yet planners do better than nonplanners. Research supports these statements, as planning is an important management skill,[2] and there is a link between planning and performance.[3]

This chapter focuses on improving your planning skills in your personal and professional lives. In this section, we explore planning dimensions, strategic versus

Effective Planning

Indicate how well each statement describes your behavior by placing a number from 1 (*does not describe me*) to 5 (*describes me*) on the line before the statement.

5	4	3	2	1
Describes me				Does not describe me

_____ 1. I have a specific result to accomplish whenever I start a project of any kind.

_____ 2. When setting objectives, I state only the result to be accomplished; I don't specify how the result will be accomplished.

_____ 3. I have specific and measurable objectives; for example, I know the specific grade I want to earn in this course.

_____ 4. I set objectives that are difficult but achievable.

_____ 5. I set deadlines when I have something I need to accomplish, and I meet the deadlines.

_____ 6. I have a long-term goal (what I will be doing in 3 to 5 years) and short-term objectives to get me there.

_____ 7. I have written objectives stating what I want to accomplish.

_____ 8. I know my strengths and weaknesses, am aware of threats, and seek opportunities.

_____ 9. I analyze a problem and alternative actions rather than immediately jumping right in with a solution.

_____10. I spend most of my day doing what I plan to do rather than dealing with emergencies and trying to get organized.

_____11. I use a calendar, appointment book, or some form of "to-do" list.

_____12. I ask others for advice.

_____13. I follow appropriate policies, procedures, and rules.

_____14. I develop contingency plans in case my plans do not work out as I expect them to.

_____15. I implement my plans and determine if I have met my objectives.

Add up the numbers you assigned to the statements to see where you fall on the continuum below.

75	65	55	45	35	25	15
Effective Planner						Ineffective Planner

Don't be too disappointed if your score isn't as high as you would like. All of these items are characteristics of effective planning. Review the items that did not describe you. After studying this chapter and doing the exercises, you can improve your planning skills.

operational planning and strategies, and the strategic planning process. Before we begin, complete Self-Assessment 5-1 to determine how well you plan.

Planning Dimensions

Planning has several dimensions. Exhibit 5-1 summarizes the five planning dimensions. Note that upper-level and some middle-level managers spend more time developing strategic, broad/directional, long-range, single-use plans for the organization.[4] Other middle-level and all lower-level managers, in contrast, spend more time specifying how the strategic plans will be accomplished[5] by developing operational, narrow/specific, short-range plans and implementing standing plans (policies, procedures, and rules). Throughout this chapter, we explore these five planning dimensions.

EXHIBIT 5-1

Planning Dimensions

MANAGEMENT LEVEL	TYPE OF PLAN	SCOPE	TIME	REPETITIVENESS
Upper and Middle	Strategic	Broad/Directional	Long Range	Single-Use Plan
Middle and Lower	Operational	Narrow/Specific	Short Range	Standing Plan

Strategic Versus Operational Planning

strategic planning The process of developing a mission and long-range objectives and determining in advance how they will be accomplished.

There are two types of plans. Strategic planning *is the process of developing a mission and long-range objectives and determining in advance how they will be accomplished.* Operational planning *is the process of setting short-range objectives and determining in advance how they will be accomplished.*

As shown in Exhibit 5-1, differences between strategic planning and operational planning are primarily the time frame and management level involved. *Long term* generally means it will take longer than one year to achieve the objective. Strategic plans are commonly developed for five years and reviewed and revised every year so that a five-year plan is always in place, such as at **Domino's. Ferrari** has an ambitious five-year growth plan to unlock the value of its sports-car brand.[6] Conversely, operational plans have short-term objectives that will be met in one year or less.

operational planning The process of setting short-range objectives and determining in advance how they will be accomplished.

At **Starbucks**, the decisions to expand by opening new stores and upscale coffee shops, going into overseas markets, and selling its products in grocery stores are all examples of strategic, long-term planning. Operational plans at Starbucks include short-term objectives developed for individual stores, such as an annual sales forecast or marketing plan for a specific location developed by a store manager or regional manager.

Strategic and Operational Strategies

strategy A plan for pursuing a mission and achieving objectives.

A strategy *is a plan for pursuing a mission and achieving objectives.* It is important to develop strategic management competency.[7] Strategic and operational types of plans include three *planning levels*: corporate, business, and functional. Each of these levels of planning requires strategies, which should be stated simply. The corporate and business levels are part of strategic planning, and the functional level is part of operational planning.

A *corporate strategy* is the strategic plan for managing multiple lines of business. In essence, there is more than one business within the corporation. A *business strategy* is the strategic plan for managing one line of business. Functional strategies are part of operational planning. A *functional strategy* is the operational plan for managing one area of a business, including operations to make the products and marketing to sell the products.

EXHIBIT 5-2

Strategic and Operational Planning and Strategies

Management Level	Planning Level	Planning Strategy/Time Range
Upper	Corporate Strategy	Strategic/Long
Upper and Middle	Business Strategy	Strategic/Long
Middle and Lower	Functional Strategy	Operational/Short

Operations   Marketing   Finance   Human Resources   Others

Exhibit 5-2 illustrates the relationship between strategic planning and operational planning and their three planning levels. We will discuss the various types of corporate, business, and functional strategies in separate sections later. The plans at the three levels must be coordinated through the strategic planning process, and adapt to changing environments.

WORK APPLICATION 5-1

Give an example of a strategic objective and an operational objective from an organization you work for or have worked for.

The Strategic Planning Process

You need to plan carefully before making a strategic move, so follow steps in the strategy planning process.[8] The steps in the *strategic planning process* are illustrated in Exhibit 5-3. Notice that the process is not simply linear; it does not proceed through steps 1 through 5 and then end. As the arrows indicate, you may need to return to prior steps and make changes as part of an ongoing process. The strategic planning process steps are included in major headings throughout the rest of this chapter.

EXHIBIT 5-3

The Strategic Planning Process

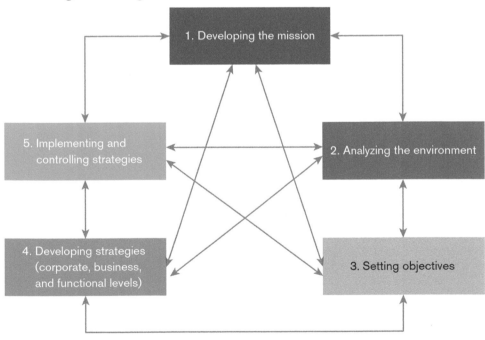

DEVELOPING THE MISSION AND
ANALYZING THE ENVIRONMENT

>> **LO 5-2:   Explain the reason for conducting an industry, competitive, and company situation analysis.**

In this section, we discuss the first and second steps of the strategic planning process.

Developing the Mission

Recall our discussion of the mission statement in Chapter 2, stating that the mission is a business's purpose or reason for being and that the firm needs the proper *organizational culture* to live the mission; so we'll be brief here. Developing the mission is the first step in the strategic planning process and the strategies developed need to reflect the culture for the strategies to be successfully implemented. However, after analyzing the environment, managers should reexamine the mission and cultural values to see if they need to be changed as the environment changes. The mission is the foundation of the other four steps in the strategic planning process.

To this end, **United Parcel Service (UPS)** has a new slogan to redefine itself as "United Problem Solvers" to reflect its new emphasis on providing global supply chain services, including **UPS Stores** and **UPS eFulfillment.** It offers multichannel inventory and ordering solutions along with shipping services.[9] **FedEx** has **FedEx Office** stores, and is focusing on business tips, marketing strategies, e-commerce solutions, and more through its **FedEx Small Business Center.**[10]

A mission is often based on or also creates a *vision* that defines where the company is headed in inventing its future and why. It contains the expectations the organization strives to achieve. However, it's not easy, as companies including **Airbnb** struggled to define its mission and brand, and **Twitter** to define a clear vision.[11]

The mission statement of the **UFC (IOM 1)** is "to help and promote the sport of MMA in order to evolve it into a major world sport." This appears to be a reasonably effective mission statement as it focuses on establishing MMA on a global level so growth is a key emphasis.

Analyzing the Environment

The second step of the strategic planning process is analyzing the environment to keep up with changes that require shifts in strategy to realign the firm's resource base in response to changes in the environment.[12] It is also known as situation analysis. A situation analysis *focuses on those features in a company's environment that most directly affect its options and opportunities.* This analysis has three parts: industry and competitive situation analysis, company situation analysis, and identification of a competitive advantage. It is important to do a good analysis, because managers tend to mis-specify what they actually face. Keep in mind that companies with multiple lines of business must conduct an environmental analysis for each line of business.

situation analysis An analysis of those features in a company's environment that most directly affect its options and opportunities.

Industry and Competitive Situation Analysis

Industries vary widely in their makeup, competitive situation, and growth potential. Determining the position of an industry requires answering questions such as these: "How large is the market?" "What is the growth rate?" "How many competitors are there?" According to **Michael Porter**, competition in an industry is a composite of five competitive forces that should be considered in analyzing the competitive situation.[13] **UPS** is struggling with profitability as giant e-tailers like **Amazon.com** command bigger discounts for deliveries and are delivering goods themselves, so it is focusing on other higher-margin services.[14] Exhibit 5-4 shows a competitive analysis for **UFC** explaining each of the five forces. Note that you start in the middle.

WORK APPLICATION 5-2

Conduct a simple five-force competitive analysis for a company you work for or have worked for. Use Exhibit 5-4 as an example.

Company Situation Analysis

A company situation analysis is used at the business level to determine the strategic issues and problems that need to be addressed through the next three steps of the

EXHIBIT 5-4

UFC's Five-Force Competitive Analysis

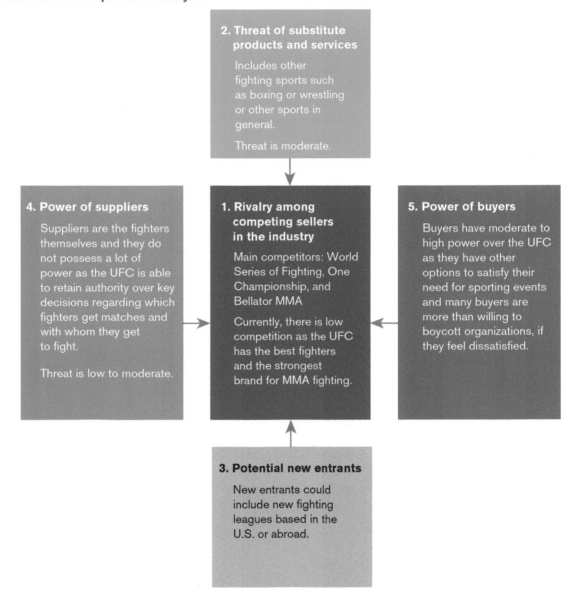

2. Threat of substitute products and services

Includes other fighting sports such as boxing or wrestling or other sports in general.

Threat is moderate.

4. Power of suppliers

Suppliers are the fighters themselves and they do not possess a lot of power as the UFC is able to retain authority over key decisions regarding which fighters get matches and with whom they get to fight.

Threat is low to moderate.

1. Rivalry among competing sellers in the industry

Main competitors: World Series of Fighting, One Championship, and Bellator MMA

Currently, there is low competition as the UFC has the best fighters and the strongest brand for MMA fighting.

5. Power of buyers

Buyers have moderate to high power over the UFC as they have other options to satisfy their need for sporting events and many buyers are more than willing to boycott organizations, if they feel dissatisfied.

3. Potential new entrants

New entrants could include new fighting leagues based in the U.S. or abroad.

strategic planning process. A complete company situation analysis has five key parts, listed in Exhibit 5-5:

1. *Assessment of the present strategy based on performance.* This assessment can be a simple statement or a more complex comparison of performance indicators (market share, sales, net profit, return on assets, and so on) over the last five years.

2. *SWOT analysis. An organization's internal environmental strengths and weaknesses and external environmental opportunities and threats are determined through a* SWOT analysis. (SWOT stands for *strengths, weaknesses, opportunities,* and *threats.*) In the critical tool SWOT analysis, the internal environmental factors analyzed for *strengths* and *weaknesses* are management and culture, mission, resources, systems, process, and structure. The external environmental (Chapter 2) factors analyzed for *opportunities* and *threats* are customers, competitors, suppliers, and so on. Focusing on opportunities is critical for firm performance.[15] Exhibit 5-6 outlines a SWOT analysis for **Starbucks**.

SWOT analysis A determination of an organization's internal environmental strengths and weaknesses and external environmental opportunities and threats.

EXHIBIT 5-5

Parts of a Company Situation Analysis

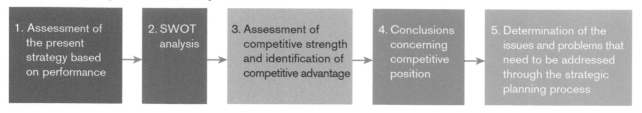

1. Assessment of the present strategy based on performance → 2. SWOT analysis → 3. Assessment of competitive strength and identification of competitive advantage → 4. Conclusions concerning competitive position → 5. Determination of the issues and problems that need to be addressed through the strategic planning process

EXHIBIT 5-6

SWOT Analysis for Starbucks

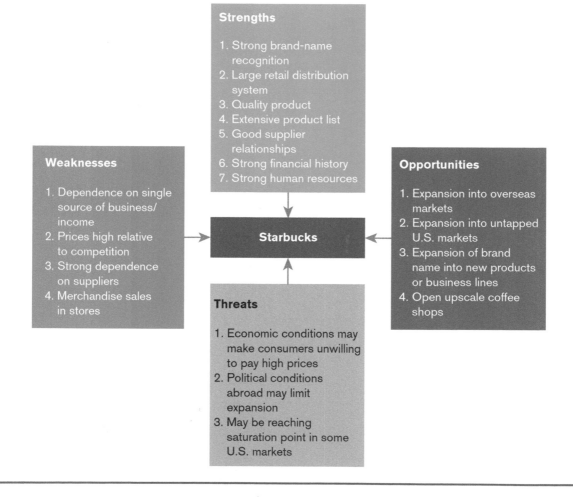

Strengths
1. Strong brand-name recognition
2. Large retail distribution system
3. Quality product
4. Extensive product list
5. Good supplier relationships
6. Strong financial history
7. Strong human resources

Weaknesses
1. Dependence on single source of business/income
2. Prices high relative to competition
3. Strong dependence on suppliers
4. Merchandise sales in stores

Starbucks

Opportunities
1. Expansion into overseas markets
2. Expansion into untapped U.S. markets
3. Expansion of brand name into new products or business lines
4. Open upscale coffee shops

Threats
1. Economic conditions may make consumers unwilling to pay high prices
2. Political conditions abroad may limit expansion
3. May be reaching saturation point in some U.S. markets

3. *Assessment of competitive strength and identification of competitive advantage.* In assessing competitive strength, you compare the *critical success factors* for a business to those of each major competitor. Critical success factors are the few major things the business must do well to be successful. We will discuss competitive advantage shortly.

4. *Conclusions concerning competitive position.* How is the business doing compared to its competition? Are things improving or slipping?

5. *Determination of the issues and problems that need to be addressed through the strategic planning process.* Based on the results of the first four parts of the company situation analysis, what needs to be done in the future to improve the business's competitive position?

6. There are many environmental factors that the **UFC (IOM 2)** must consider in relation to its planning process. For example, it needs to identify which countries have customers that would be interested in the UFC. Countries such as China, Germany, France, and Singapore are examples of countries with large numbers of potential fans. Another factor would be legal factors. Are there any countries that have laws and regulations that may restrict UFC tournaments? A third example would be technological factors. For example, does Wi-Fi service exist in various countries to support video streaming of matches through various mobile devices?

Competitive Advantage

A competitive advantage *specifies how an organization offers unique customer value.* It answers the questions, "What makes us different from and better than the competition?" and "Why should a person buy our products rather than those of our competitors?" A company has to have answers to these questions to have a sustainable competitive advantage and succeed in business. A firm may identify a competitive advantage in the process of assessing its competitive strength. Many companies, including **Wegmans,** say their people are their advantage.[16] **Starbucks**'s competitive advantage is its relaxed coffee house environment where friends can meet that offers high-quality coffee and other products.

UFC's **(IOM 3)** competitive advantage is that it has partnerships with other fighting leagues and it possesses the strongest stable of world class MMA fighters including some superstars such as **Rhonda Rousey** (former star) and **Conor McGregor.** Whether the UFC can sustain its competitive advantage is unclear as consumer preferences and interests may change over time. This is of particular concern with younger fans from Generation Y and Z. New sports leagues may also emerge that challenge the UFC in the future as well. With so much uncertainty in the external environment, it is difficult to predict whether the UFC will be able to sustain its popularity and profitability.

Two aspects of a company's competitive advantage are core competency and benchmarking. A *core competency* is what a firm does well. By identifying core competencies, managers can oversee the creation of new products and services that take advantage of the company's strengths. **TGI Fridays** determined its core competency to be selling and managing franchisees, not operating restaurants. So it will sell most of its 200-plus U.S. and UK company-owned restaurants to franchisees.[17]

Benchmarking is the process of comparing an organization's products or services and processes with those of other companies. In benchmarking, you try to find out about other products and processes, through competitive intelligence, and copy them or improve upon them legally and ethically. Most benchmarking takes place within an industry. The Internet is an excellent source of information for benchmarking.

Pizza Hut, Papa John's, and **Little Caesars** copied **Domino's** delivery. However, looking at noncompetitors can provide good ideas that create a competitive advantage. Many other restaurants now have similar delivery models. **Uber** and **Airbnb** have inspired copycats and other types of businesses.

competitive advantage Specifies how an organization offers unique customer value.

benchmarking The process of comparing an organization's products and services and processes with those of other companies.

Changing Strategies

After managers have evaluated the organization and the competition by completing the situation analysis, they should go back and review the mission and its vision to see if these need to be changed. Remember that situation analysis is an ongoing process, referred to as *scanning the environment.* It tells what is going on in the external environment that may require change to continually improve customer value. **Netflix** changed its business model from shipping DVDs to streaming to creating original programming to stream.

Domino's **model of quick ordering and delivery has become a process that many other pizza delivery companies benchmark.**

©iStockphoto.com/jaminwell

SETTING OBJECTIVES

>> **LO 5-3:** **State the criteria for an effectively written objective by identifying must and want criteria.**

After developing a mission and completing a situation analysis, you are ready for the third step in the strategic planning process: setting objectives that flow from the mission to take advantage of opportunities and address problems identified through the situation analysis. In this section, we discuss writing objectives, criteria for effective objectives, and management by objectives (MBO).

Writing Effective Objectives

objectives Statements of what is to be accomplished that are expressed in singular, specific, and measurable terms with a target date.

Although it is common to use the terms goals and objectives as having the same definition, you should be able to distinguish between goals and objectives. *Goals* state general, broad targets to be accomplished. Objectives *state what is to be accomplished in specific and measurable terms with a target date.* Recall that objectives are end results; they do not state how they will be accomplished—that's the plan.[18] Having goals is important,[19] because setting objectives and planning are among the most important drivers of performance.[20]

To help ensure that you will meet your objectives, it is a good idea to write them down and review them. Entrepreneur and *Shark Tank* TV star **Daymond John** is goal driven and reads his list of objectives every morning.[21] You will practice setting objectives in Skill Builder 5-1.

Max E. Douglas, Indiana State University, developed a model that is helpful in writing effective objectives. One variation on Douglas's model is shown in Model 5-1, with some examples of corporate strategic objectives shown following the model.

MODEL 5-1

Setting Objectives

(1) *To* + (2) Action Verb + (3) Specific and Measurable Result + (4) Target Date

Corporate Objectives Using the Model

Nike: To (2) hit annual sales of $50 billion by 2020.[22]

Ford: To (2) sell (3) driverless cars without steering wheels or pedals by (4) 2021.[23]

Aldi: To have 2,500 stores by the end of 2022.[24]

Exxon: To increase oil output 25% by 2025.[25]

GM: To sell two million cars a year through 2030.[26]

Criteria for Objectives

As the model for writing objectives implies, an effective objective conforms to three "must" criteria: It expresses a *specific* and *measurable*[27] result, and it sets a *date* (deadline) for achieving that result.[28] It should also have a single result—or don't put multiple objectives together. Another similar way of writing objectives is called *SMART goals*—specific, measurable, attainable, realistic, and timely.

Let's discuss the parts of Model 5-1, or the criteria that needed to be met in the model. Note that as shown in Exhibit 5-7, the top or first three are "must" criteria, as they are required for writing effective objectives, whereas the bottom or last three are "want" criteria because it can't be known if they are met by reading the objective.

Difficult but Achievable (Realistic)

A number of studies show that individuals perform better when given difficult but achievable (realistic) objectives rather than objectives that are too difficult (don't try)

EXHIBIT 5-7

Criteria That Objectives Should Meet

Specific. Vague objectives fail.[a] So objectives should state the exact level of performance desired.[b] Specific objectives lead to focus on achieving them.[c]

Ineffective Objective	To maximize profits in 2020 (How much is "maximize"?)
Effective Objective	To earn a net profit of $1 million in 2020

Measurable. If you are to achieve objectives, you must be able to observe and measure progress regularly to determine if the objectives have been met.[d]

Ineffective Objective	Perfect service for every customer (How is "perfect service" measured?)
Effective Objective	To attain an "excellent" satisfaction rating from 90% of customers surveyed in 2020

Target Date. A specific date should be set for accomplishing the objective. When people have a deadline, they usually try harder to get a task done on time than when they are simply told to do it when they can.

Ineffective Objective	To become a millionaire (by when?)
Effective Objective	To become a millionaire by December 31, 2020

It is also more effective to set a specific date than to give a time span, because it's too easy to forget when a time period began and should end.

Somewhat Effective	To double international business to $5 billion annually within five years
Effective Objective	To double international business to $5 billion annually by year-end 2019

Note, however, that some objectives are ongoing and do not require a stated date. The target date is indefinite until it is changed.

Somewhat Effective	To be number one or two in world sales in all lines of business—**GM**
Effective Objective	To have 25% of sales coming from products that did not exist five years ago—**3M**

a. H. Mitchell, "What's the Best Way to Stick With a Resolution?" *The Wall Street Journal* (December 23, 2014): D1, D2.
b. R. Bachman, "The Week Your New Year's Resolution to Exercise Dies," *The Wall Street Journal* (January 19, 2015): D1, D4.
c. M. Dorf, "Long-Distance Leadership," *Entrepreneur* (March 2015): 19.
d. H. Ibarra, "The Way to Become a Strategic Executive," *The Wall Street Journal* (February 23, 2015): R7.

or too easy (do the minimum). But be aware that too difficult an objective can lead to not trying or unethical behavior to achieve it to attain the reward for doing so or avoid a punishment—like at **Wells Fargo**. You want to have stretch objectives.[29] Olympic gold medalist **Dorothy Hamill** said to push yourself to strive for the highest standards of achievement. Here is a tip. The longer you give yourself to achieve an objective, the longer it will take. So set a false/earlier deadline. It will force you to get more done.[30] **Apple's Steve Jobs** was known for motivationally pushing employees to complete what seemed unrealistic or impossible objectives.

5-1 JOIN THE DISCUSSION • ETHICS & SOCIAL RESPONSIBILITY

 Objectives

Objectives should be difficult but achievable. However, **Wells Fargo & Co.** is considered to have created objectives that were too difficult and led to bank employees feeling pressured by the quotas and managers' pressure to meet the objectives. The pressure resulted in employees creating "new

accounts" that customers never asked for, either to keep their jobs or to get more sales commissions. This practice resulted in overdraft fees for customers. The government imposed a fine of $185 million, and CEO **John Stumpf** retired.

Mary Mack, senior executive vice president of community banking at **Wells Fargo**, was tasked with coming up with a new incentive system that didn't result

(Continued)

(Continued)

in unethical or illegal activities on the part of its 100,000 retail-bank employees at some 6,000 U.S. branches. Mack said Wells Fargo won't abandon cross-selling, or efforts to sell multiple products to individual households, which was seen as contributing to the misconduct.

1. If you were a manager at Wells Fargo, would you pressure employees?

2. Would you fire employees who didn't meet the difficult quotas?

3. As an employee, would you give in to the pressure and use unethical/illegal practices to meet the quotas in order to keep your job?

4. As an employee, would you use unethical practices to exceed the quotas in order to make more money?

5. Would your answers to questions 3 and 4 change if you knew it was common practice of your coworkers to use these techniques and encourage you to do the same things? How about if there was peer pressure to also use the tactics?

Source: A. Andriotis and E. Glazer, "Wells Fargo Managers Pushed Overdraft Services," *The Wall Street Journal* (October 10, 2016): C1, C2; E. Glazer, "Can She Save Wells Fargo's Branches?" *The Wall Street Journal* (October 20, 2016): C1, C2.

Participatively Set

Groups that participate in setting their objectives generally outperform groups with assigned objectives; participation helps members feel they have a shared destiny. Managers say they do at least get input when setting company objectives. You should use the appropriate level of participation for the employees' capabilities (Chapters 1 and 4).

Acceptance and Commitment

It is important to get the acceptance and support of important stakeholders that will achieve the objective.[31] If employees do not commit to an objective, then even if it meets all the other "must" and "want" criteria, it may not be accomplished. So you want to get people thinking and believing "I can do that" to motivate them to achieve the objective.[32]

> **WORK APPLICATION 5-3**
>
> *Using the model for writing objectives, write one or more objectives for an organization you work for or have worked for, making sure they meet the "must" criteria.*

Management by Objectives (MBO)

management by objectives (MBO) The process in which managers and their employees jointly set objectives for the employees, periodically evaluate performance, and reward according to the results.

Management by objectives (MBO) is the process in which managers and their employees jointly set objectives for the employees, periodically evaluate performance, and reward according to the results, and it is used at firms including by athletic coaches at **Springfield College**.[33] At **Google**, every employee has objectives, and every other employee can see them.[34] MBO is also referred to as work planning and review, goals management, goals and controls, and management by results.

MBO has three steps:

Step 1. Set individual objectives and plans. You set objectives with each individual employee. The objectives are the heart of the MBO process and should meet the "must" and "want" criteria. They should be based on achieving the company and team objectives.

Step 2. Give feedback and evaluate performance. Communication is the key factor in determining MBO's success or failure. Thus, you and your employees must meet frequently to review progress. The frequency of evaluations depends on the individual and the job performed.

Step 3. Reward according to performance. Employees' performance should be measured against their objectives. Employees who meet their objectives should be rewarded through recognition, praise, pay raises, promotions, and so on. We will discuss motivating employees with rewards in Chapter 11 and measuring performance in Chapter 14.

5-1 APPLYING THE CONCEPT

Objectives

For each objective, state which "must" criterion is not met.

- A. single result
- B. specific
- C. measurable
- D. target date

___ 1. To complete the project within two weeks.

___ 2. To be perceived as the highest quality hotel in the tri-state area by the end of 2030

___ 3. To write objectives next week

___ 4. To double profits in Mexico

___ 5. To sell 10% more nachos and 5% more beer at the hockey game on February 20, 2020

___ 6. To increase sales in 2030

CORPORATE-LEVEL STRATEGIES

>> **LO 5-4:** **Discuss corporate-level strategies in terms of the four grand strategies and the three growth strategies.**

To achieve your objectives, you move on to the fourth step of the strategic planning process: developing strategies at the corporate, business, and functional levels. In this section, we discuss corporate strategies, which are shown in Exhibit 5-8. Recall that to have a corporate strategy, the parent corporation must have subsidiary or business unit companies (companies within one company). So a corporate strategy allocates and coordinates resources among its different business units.

EXHIBIT 5-8

Grand and Growth Strategies

```
                          Grand Strategy
        ┌──────────────┬──────────────┬──────────────┐
        ▼              ▼              ▼              ▼
    Growth         Stability    Turnaround and    Combination
(aggressively   (remain the    Retrenchment    (mix of other three)
 expand size)    same or       (reverse a
                 grow slowly)  negative trend
                               and cut back)
        │
        ▼
              Growth Strategies
Concentration—expand existing line(s) of business
Integration—expand forward and/or backward within line(s) of business
Diversification—add related and/or unrelated products
```

A diversification strategy at the corporate level entails selling a variety of products and/or services. Samsung **sells electronics and appliances, but it also operates the Everland amusement park in South Korea.**

©iStockphoto.com/HotDuckZ

grand strategy An overall corporate strategy for growth, stability, or turnaround and retrenchment, or for some combination of these.

Grand Strategy

A critical role of CEOs of multibusiness MNCs is to develop a grand strategy.[35] A **grand strategy** *is an overall corporate strategy for growth, stability, or turnaround and retrenchment, or for some combination of these.* Each grand strategy aligns with different objectives. Let's discuss each separately.

Growth

With a *growth strategy,* the company makes aggressive attempts to increase its size through increased sales, and companies using this strategy include **Amazon, Google,** and **Facebook.** The 24-hour fitness club **Anytime Fitness** hit the 3,000-unit milestone faster than **Subway, McDonald's,** or **Dunkin' Donuts.**[36]

Stability

With a *stability strategy,* the company attempts to hold and maintain its present size or to grow slowly. Many smaller companies are satisfied with the status quo, but large MNCs are expected to keep growing. Rather than increasing its size aggressively, the company attempts to balance growth and profits. The **WD-40 Company** produces WD-40 lubricant. The company pursues a strategy of stability, as it has gradually added products over the years.[37]

Turnaround and Retrenchment

A *turnaround strategy* is an attempt to reverse a declining business as quickly as possible. Led largely by a female management team, **Best Buy** completed a difficult turnaround and is now profitable.[38] A *retrenchment strategy* is the divestiture or liquidation of assets. These strategies are listed together because most turnarounds include retrenchment. Turnaround strategies generally attempt to improve cash flow by increasing revenues, decreasing costs, reducing assets, or combining these strategies to realign the firm with its external environment. **GE** is selling business lines.[39] **Ford** is stopping or has stopped production of its Fiesta, C-MAX, Taurus, Focus, and Fusion.[40] Most retail chains are closing all stores (**Limited, Payless**) or some stores (**Macy's, JCPenney**).[41] **Starbucks** plans to close 150 U.S. cafés.[42]

A *spinoff* is a form of retrenchment in which a corporation sets up one or more of its business units as a separate company rather than selling it. **KFC** spun off its China stores. **Xerox** split into two companies. **Pfizer** and **Honeywell** are spinning off major business units to focus on their core operations.[43]

Combination

Corporations may pursue growth, stability, and turnaround and retrenchment for their different lines of business or areas of operations, which are considered business-level strategies, discussed shortly, but they tend to have one overall corporate strategy.

WORK APPLICATION 5-4

State the grand strategy for an organization you work for or have worked for.

Growth Strategies

Most large MNCs have growth strategies, and that is a major reason they are global MNCs. A company that wants to grow has three major options. These **growth strategies** *are concentration, backward and forward integration, and related and unrelated diversification.*

Concentration

With a *concentration strategy*, the organization grows aggressively in its existing line(s) of business. **Starbucks** has a concentration growth strategy to continue to open new company owned stores globally, as do most franchisors. **Smoothie King** started with one location and is currently franchised with rapid growth and plans to open 125 locations and bring the number of its global stores to 950.[44]

Integration

With an *integration strategy*, the organization enters a new line or lines of business related to its existing one(s) on a continuum as follows:

Raw Materials, Farms	Manufacturing	Retail, Wholesale	Customer
←Backward Integration	←————————————→		Forward Integration→

Forward integration occurs when the organization enters a line of business closer to the final customer. **Apple** (manufacturing) has engaged in forward integration by opening **Apple Stores** (retail), thus bypassing traditional retailers. **CVS** is bringing one-stop shopping to Health Care.[45] CVS acquired **Aetna** to create a vertical integrated health-care system that is transforming the way America goes to the doctor. Aetna insurance will bring customers to 9,700 CVS stores that will include **MinuteClinics** to provide health care and pharmacy services to improve the quality and lower the cost of health care.[46] *Backward integration* occurs when the organization enters a line of business farther away from the final customer. **Delta Airlines** (retail service) bought a refinery (manufacturing) to lower its jet-fuel costs. **Coca-Cola** (primarily makes the concentrate) bought several of its bottling and distribution manufacturers, moving toward customers with a growth strategy, but sold several of them, moving backwards with a retrenchment strategy.[47]

Diversification

With a *diversification strategy*, the organization goes into a related or unrelated line of products, and this growth strategy can be risky.[48] **Apple** seeks new growth beyond its iPhone and is promoting its **Apple TV Plus** with video streaming of original content, news, TV app, Game Services,[49] and the **Apple Card**; a credit card with **Goldman Sachs** paired with iPhone features to help manage your money.[50] **Nike** used *related (concentric) diversification* when it diversified from sports shoes to sports clothing and then to sports equipment. **Dunkin' Donuts** and **Starbucks** selling products in grocery stores was a related diversification strategy. **Coca-Cola** is diversifying away from its soda roots[51] with the related theme, "Beverages for Life" by offering all types of people at all stages of their lives and for a variety of purposes. Coke has 500 brands and 3,500 products (including **Dasani, Powerade, Minute Maid, Gold Peak, Costa Coffee,** and **Honest Tea**) around the world.[52]

Virgin Group has pursued an unrelated (conglomerate) diversification since its existence, owning several ventures in the following industries: entertainment, health and wellness, leisure, money, people and planet, space, telecom and tech, and travel.[53] Did you know that **Mars**, the candy maker, is also in the pet-care industry? Its affiliate brands include **Pedigree, Iams, Royal Canin**, and, more recently, **VCA Animal Hospitals**.[54]

Merger and Acquisition Growth Strategy

Companies can also pursue a common MNC growth strategy by means of mergers and acquisitions, commonly referred to as M&As. Companies engage in M&As to decrease competition, to compete more effectively with larger companies, to realize economies of size, to consolidate expenses, and to achieve access to markets, products, technology, resources, and management talent. Since 2012, conglomerate **JAB Holdings** has grown by spending over $57 billion to acquire **Dr. Pepper Snapple, Keurig Green Mountain, Panera Bread, Krispy Kreme,** and four other coffee companies.[55]

A **merger** *occurs when two companies form one corporation.* The new company name is often a combination of the merged businesses. **Anheuser-Busch** and **InBev** merged to create **Anheuser-Busch InBev**, creating the leading global beer brewer. A merger between **Coopers & Lybrand** and **Price Waterhouse** became **PricewaterhouseCoopers.**

The **UFC (IOM 4)** appears to be pursuing a combination of a growth strategy and a merger and acquisition strategy. It is growing organically by expanding the venues it uses for tournaments around the United States and further leveraging cable and pay-per-view deals. On a global level, it is also growing through acquisitions of fighting leagues in countries like Japan.

An **acquisition** *occurs when one business buys all or part of another business.* One business becomes a part of an existing business. **Google** bought **Motorola. Facebook** acquired **Instagram. Microsoft** acquired **LinkedIn. Marriott** bought **Starwood Hotels.**

The terms *merger* and *acquisition* are commonly used interchangeably. However, with a true merger, owners of stock in each company get new shares in the new combined company under its new name. With a true acquisition, stock owners in the acquired company get shares in its purchaser stock. When **Google** acquired **YouTube**, its stock owners got Google shares. Despite their popularity, M&As often don't lead to greater coordination, and M&As have a dismal track record, as half the deals eventually divest.[56]

Portfolio Analysis

Business portfolio analysis *is the corporate process of determining which lines of business the corporation will be in and how it will allocate resources among them.* A business line, also called a strategic business unit (SBU), is a distinct business having its own

merger Occurs when two companies form one corporation.

acquisition Occurs when one business buys all or part of another business.

business portfolio analysis The corporate process of determining which lines of business the corporation will be in and how it will allocate resources among them.

5-2 APPLYING THE CONCEPT

Growth Strategies

Identify the type of growth strategy described by each statement.

A. concentration
B. related diversification
C. forward integration
D. unrelated diversification
E. backward integration

_____ 7. PepsiCo's Sprite soda buys lemon and lime groves.

_____ 8. Dell Computer starts making printers.

_____ 9. Home Depot acquires a tool manufacturer to make its own brand-name tools.

_____ 10. Facebook buys Toys "R" Us.

_____ 11. Apple opens a new Apple store in a mall.

_____ 12. Tesla starts opening its own dealerships to sell its cars.

_____ 13. New Age Diamond Mines starts to cut its stones into diamond shapes for jewelry.

_____ 14. Pizza Hut opens one of its fast-food restaurants in China.

_____ 15. Netflix acquires a small upscale restaurant in New York.

_____ 16. Boeing buys the Johnson Custom Jets company.

 Insider Trading

Insiders are people who have confidential information about upcoming events that will affect the price of a stock. It is common for the price of a stock to go up when investors learn that the company is negotiating a merger or acquisition of another company. Insiders are not supposed to buy or sell any stock they have confidential information about or to tell anyone this information to avoid illegal profit from stock dealing. This process, known as "tipping," is illegal. However, many government public officials have access to insider information and legally get rich from tipping.

1. If you were "tipped" by an insider, would you buy/sell the stock?

2. What are the implications of using insider information? Is anyone hurt by the practice? If yes, who is hurt, and how are they hurt?

3. Without using insider information, some speculators try to predict which companies are likely to merge or be acquired and buy stock options. This is a legal way of making money, but is it ethical?

4. Is it ethical for government officials to use insider information to make money?

customers that is managed independently of other businesses within the corporation. What constitutes an SBU varies from company to company, but it can be a division, a subsidiary, or a single product line. **PepsiCo** started with just **Pepsi** and went on to acquire a business portfolio including **Frito-Lay**, **Tropicana**, **Gatorade**, and **Quaker Oats,** each of which is an SBU—or PepsiCo has multiple companies within a company with a growth grand strategy.

The primary objective of *corporate portfolio management (CPM)* is to make strategic decisions about the allocation of resources among SBUs. A popular approach to CPM is to create a **Boston Consulting Group (BCG)** Growth-Share Matrix for each line of business or product line as a business strategy. A BCG matrix contains four cells: *Cash cows* generate more resources than they need, so the profits are used to fund question marks and stars. *Question marks* are entries into new businesses. *Stars* are question marks that succeed. *Dogs* are doing poorly and are usually sold or liquidated. Exhibit 5-9 shows a BCG matrix for **UFC** (IOM 4).

EXHIBIT 5-9

BCG Growth Share Matrix for UFC

An important part of CPM is developing stars (growth) and dropping dogs (retrenchment to give resources to question marks)—which companies to buy and sell. **PepsiCo** acquired **Gatorade** and became the market leader in sports drinks, and it sold its fast-food restaurants **KFC, Pizza Hut**, and **Taco Bell** to **Yum! Brands**. However, selecting successfully is very challenging. Recall that managers have *cognitive bias* (Chapter 4) that limits their ability to collect complete data and sort through these options effectively, particularly in more dynamic environments in which the decision-making context is more complex, more ambiguous with greater risk and uncertainty.[57] **GE** is currently in retrenchment and has to select which SBU to sell.

A company in a single line of business cannot conduct a business portfolio analysis. However, it should perform a *product portfolio analysis*. **McDonald's** started by offering a simple hamburger and fries. Over the years, the company introduced new products, such as the Big Mac and salads, that started as a question mark, became a star, and then joined the hamburger and fries as a cash cow. McDonald's introduced pizza and the Angus Burger as question marks, but rather than becoming stars, they became dogs and were dropped from most restaurants.

BUSINESS-LEVEL STRATEGIES

>> **LO 5-5:** **Summarize the three business-level adaptive and competitive strategies.**

Each line of business must develop its own mission, analyze its own environment, set its own objectives, and develop its own strategies. For the organization with a single line of products, corporate and business strategies are the same, so we are still in the fourth step of the strategic planning process. In this section, we discuss adaptive and competitive strategies.

Adaptive Strategies

adaptive strategies Overall strategies for a line of business, including prospecting, defending, and analyzing.

Adaptive strategies emphasize adapting to changes in the external environment and entering new markets as a means of increasing sales. The **adaptive strategies** *are prospecting, defending,* and *analyzing*. Each adaptive strategy reflects a different objective. Exhibit 5-10 indicates the different rates of environmental change, potential growth rates, and corresponding grand strategy for each adaptive strategy.

Prospecting Strategy

The *prospecting strategy* calls for aggressively offering new products and services and/or entering new markets in pursuit of opportunities.[58] The prospecting strategy resembles the grand strategy of growth, and prospecting firms tend to be the most successful. It is often used by smaller companies that want to grow fast, like **Groupon**, which was one of the fastest-growing startup prospectors of all times.[59]

EXHIBIT 5-10

Adaptive Strategies

ADAPTIVE STRATEGY	RATE OF ENVIRONMENTAL CHANGE	POTENTIAL GROWTH RATE	POTENTIAL GROWTH RATE
Prospecting	Fast	High	Growth
Analyzing and Imitation	Moderate	Moderate	Combination
Defending	Slow	Low	Stability

Defending Strategy

The *defending strategy* calls for staying with the present product line and markets and maintaining or increasing customers slowly in new markets. It is often used by large established companies that want to protect their dominance, like **Coca-Cola** keeping its number-one position against archrival **Pepsi**. The defending strategy resembles the grand strategy of stability.

Analyzing and Imitation Strategy

The *analyzing strategy* calls for a midrange approach between prospecting and defending. Analyzing resembles the combination grand strategy. Analyzing involves moving into new market areas at a cautious, deliberate pace and/or offering a core product group and seeking new opportunities.

Analyzers also commonly copy their rivals' prospecting actions using an *imitation strategy*.[60] **Domino's** was the prospector offering pizza delivery first. **Pizza Hut** was the analyzer waiting to see if delivery would be successful, and when it was, Pizza Hut copied Domino's. **Miller** was the first to offer a successful light beer, so **AB** came out with **Bud Light**.

WORK APPLICATION 5-5

Identify the adaptive strategy used by an organization you work for or have worked for. Be sure to describe how it used the strategy.

Competitive Strategies

Michael Porter identified three effective business *competitive strategies*: differentiation, cost leadership, and focus.[61]

Differentiation Strategy

With a *differentiation* strategy, a company stresses its competitive advantage over its competitors, focusing on being sufficiently distinctive. Differentiation strategy somewhat resembles the prospecting strategy and tends to lead to being able to charge

---

5-3 APPLYING THE CONCEPT

Adaptive Strategies

Identify the type of strategy represented in each statement.

A. prospecting
B. defending
C. analyzing

_____ 17. Dell pioneers a laptop-powered computer that can be folded up to the size of a smartphone.

_____ 18. Domino's used this strategy after Pizza Hut started to copy delivering pizza.

_____ 19. This is the primary strategy of Walmart in the saturated U.S. market as the number of dollar stores increased.

_____ 20. When McDonald's came out with a new Angus Burger to compete with Burger King's successful Angus Burgers, it was using this strategy.

_____ 21. 7-Eleven expands globally by opening stores in Vietnam.

The distinct look of a Coca-Cola **label is part of the company's differentiation strategy.**

©iStockphoto.com/
BlakeDavidTaylor

higher prices than competitors, such as **Apple** iPhone over **Samsung** Galaxy. **Adidas, Ralph Lauren, Calvin Klein**, and others place their names and logos on the outside of their products to differentiate them. **Coca-Cola** uses differentiation with its scripted name logo and contour bottle.

Cost Leadership Strategy

With a *cost leadership* strategy, the company stresses lower prices to attract customers. To keep its prices down, it must have tight cost control and efficient low-cost systems processes. Growth demands high volume, and high volume demands low prices. **Walmart** and **Target** have had success with this strategy. Some firms start with a low cost strategy and change as they grow.[62] **Southwest** has changed its low-cost strategy. **Allegiant, Spirit**, and **JetBlue** have become today's low-cost carriers.

Focus Strategy

With a *focus strategy*, the company targets a specific regional market, product line, or buyer group. Within a particular target segment, or market niche, the firm may use a differentiation or cost leadership strategy. With a focus strategy, smaller companies can often compete with MNCs by not competing head on based on price. **Asics** successfully competes with much larger **Nike** and **Adidas** by focusing on the running shoe market. ***Ebony*** and ***Jet*** magazines target African Americans, and **Rolex** watches have a market niche of upper-income people. **Right Guard** deodorant is aimed at men and **Secret** at women.

Porter doesn't recommend trying to combine differentiation and cost leadership because it is rarely successful, as the company gets stuck in the middle. Remember that the various grand and adaptive strategies complement one another. Managers select the appropriate strategy based on the mission, situation analysis, and objectives.

OPERATIONAL-LEVEL PLANNING

>> **LO 5-6:   Identify strategies for short-range operational planning.**

So far in this chapter, we have discussed long-range, external, competitive strategic planning; we are at the last part of the fourth step of the planning process—operational-level planning. After selecting the strategy, you need to develop plans to achieve the objectives.[63] In this section, we discuss short-range operational planning, including functional strategies, standing and single-use plans, and contingency plans and crisis.

5-4 APPLYING THE CONCEPT

Competitive Adaptive Strategies

Identify the type of strategy used by the company listed.

    A. differentiation

    B. cost leadership

    C. focus

_____ 22. Dollar General variety store

_____ 23. Nike sports apparel

_____ 24. Nickelodeon TV network

_____ 25. Anytime Fitness exercise gym

At an operational level, the **UFC** (**IOM** 5) is focusing on putting together UFC events with appealing cards filled with great **MMA** fighters. It holds UFC events all around the country and not just in its home base of Las Vegas. It is developing its brand through its partnership with **Body Armor**, sports drinks, and opening UFC-sponsored training schools. These operational plans do appear to be in alignment with the UFC's overall goal to grow and establish MMA as a major sport around the world.

Functional Strategies

The functional departments of a company must develop internal strategic plans for achieving the mission and objectives. Functional strategies *are strategies developed and implemented by managers in marketing, operations, human resources, finance, and other departments of a company.*

functional strategies Strategies developed and implemented by managers in marketing, operations, human resources, finance, and other departments.

Marketing Strategy

The marketing department has the primary responsibility for knowing what the customer wants, or how to add customer value, and for defining the target market. Marketing focuses on the four *P*s: product, promotion, place, and price. The marketing department makes decisions about which products to provide, how they will be packaged and advertised, where they will be sold and how they will get there, and how much they will be sold for.

Operations Strategy

The operations (or production) department is responsible for systems processes that convert inputs into outputs of products or services for its customers. Operations focuses on quality and efficiency in producing the products that marketing determines will provide customer value. (You will learn more about operations in Chapter 15.)

Finance Strategy

The finance department has at least two functions: (1) financing the business activities by raising money through the sale of stock (equity) or bonds or through loans (debt) and paying off the debt and dividends (if any) to shareholders, and (2) keeping records of transactions, developing budgets, and reporting financial results (income and cash flow statements and balance sheet). (You will learn more about finance in Chapter 14.)

Human Resources Strategy

The human resources (HR) department is responsible for working with all the other functional departments in the areas of recruiting, selecting, training, evaluating, and compensating employees. (You will learn more about HR in Chapter 9.)

Other Functional Strategies

Based on the type of business, any number of other departments will also need to develop a strategy, such as internal functions like information technology (IT) and research and development (R&D).

Standing Plans Versus Single-Use Plans

Depending on how repetitive they are, plans may be either *standing plans*, which are made to be used over and over again to ensure repeated behavior for handling routine issues, or *single-use plans*, which are made to be used only once (nonrepetitive).[64] Most strategic plans are single use, whereas operational plans are more often standing plans. Exhibit 5-11 illustrates the different types of standing and single-use plans.

Standing Plans Versus Single-Use Plans

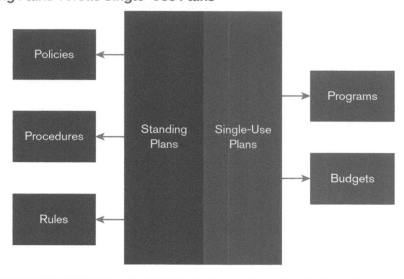

Standing Plans

Routines are a foundational concept in strategy because they explain how work is accomplished.[65] So, you need to develop efficient standing plans to develop routines to get the job done. Operational objectives may be accomplished by following standing plans, which save planning and decision-making time. **Standing plans** *are policies, procedures, and rules developed for handling repetitive situations.* Their purpose is to guide employees' actions in day-to-day decision making, such as how to communicate with customers[66] and other stakeholders within and outside the firm.

Corporations have a board of directors that have *organizational governance* structure responsibility to develop standing plans that shape the firm's actions to achieve its mission. The board establishes standing plans about who will be in charge, how leadership turnover will occur, who will be involved in major decisions, how gains will be distributed, and who will bear the risk of failure.[67] The board has power to hire and fire the CEO and other executives. **Apple**'s board fired founder **Steve Jobs.**

Policies *provide general guidelines to be followed when making decisions.* Companies should develop formal policies, as they serve as guides for employee behavior in their relationships with stakeholders. Here are a few examples of policy statements: "The customer is always right." "We produce high-quality goods and services." "We promote employees from within." Notice that policy statements are intentionally general guides; you use your discretion in implementing them. As a manager, your daily decisions will be guided by policies.

A **procedure** *is a sequence of actions to be followed in order to achieve an objective.* Procedures may also be called *standard operating procedures (SOPs)* or *methods.* Procedures can be formal or informal and are more specific than policies, as they establish routine ways of doing things consistently.[68] Procedures ensure that all recurring, routine situations are handled in a consistent, predetermined manner,[69] such as making products, purchasing, taking inventory, settling grievances, and so forth.

Rules *state exactly what should or should not be done.* Policy routines can lead to establishing rules for greater consistency of behavior, as employees have no discretion on how to implement rules and regulations designed to govern their behaviors.[70] These are examples of rules: "No smoking or eating in the work area." "Everyone must wear a hard hat on the construction site." **Google** was having incivility problems, so it set

standing plans Policies, procedures, and rules developed for handling repetitive situations.

policies General guidelines to be followed when making decisions.

procedure A sequence of actions to be followed in order to achieve an objective.

rules Statements of exactly what should or should not be done.

rules designed to limit offensive language and personal attacks among employees.[71] Violating rules usually subjects a person to penalties that vary in severity according to the seriousness of the violation and the number of offenses. You will learn how to discipline employees in Chapter 14.

WORK APPLICATION 5-6

Give an example of a policy, a procedure, and a rule from an organization you work for or have worked for.

Single-Use Plans

Single-use plans *are programs and budgets developed for handling nonrepetitive situations.* Single-use plans, unlike standing plans, are developed for a specific purpose and probably will not be used again in the same form. However, a single-use plan may be used as a model for a future version of the program or budget. A corporate- or business-level strategy is usually a single-use plan, such as a turnaround strategy, that can result in new standing plans.

A *program* describes a set of activities and is designed to accomplish an objective over a specified time period. A program may have its own policies, procedures, budget, and so forth. It might take several years or less than a day to complete a given program. Examples include the development of a new product or expansion of facilities.

A *budget* is the funds allocated to operate a unit for a fixed period. When that time has passed, a new budget is needed. Developing a budget requires planning skills rather than accounting and mathematical skills. When developed, a budget is a planning tool, and when implemented, it is a control tool. We discuss budgeting in Chapter 14.

> **single-use plans** Programs and budgets developed for handling nonrepetitive situations.

Contingency Plans and Crises

Contingency plans and crises go together because you use contingency plans to help prevent crises and to deal with crises.

5-5 APPLYING THE CONCEPT

Identifying Plans

Identify the type of plan exemplified by each statement.

  A. policy

  B. procedure

  C. rule

  D. program

  E. budget

    _____ 26. At Ford, quality is job one.

    _____ 27. A helmet must be worn on the football field.

    _____ 28. Forms for a leave of absence must be filled out, approved, and signed by the supervisor and submitted to the HR office one month in advance of the planned leave.

    _____ 29. We follow the "Humanics Philosophy" at Springfield College.

    _____ 30. We will make a driverless car within five years.

    _____ 31. Here is an Excel sheet describing how much I need to run my division next year.

Contingency Plans

No matter how effectively you plan, there will be times when probable expected events prevent you from achieving your objectives. Things that go wrong are often beyond your control.[72] When the uncontrollable occurs, you should be prepared with a backup, or contingency, plan. **Contingency plans** *are alternative plans to be implemented if uncontrollable events occur.* If a key employee calls in sick, another employee fills in to do the job. Construction work is usually contingent on the weather. If it's nice, employees work outside; if it is not, they work indoors. If a fire starts, how do you put it out and evacuate people?

Crisis

To develop a contingency plan to help prevent unexpected *crises*, answer three questions: What might go wrong? How can I prevent it from happening? If it does occur, what can I do to minimize its effect? The answer to question 3 is your contingency plan. With good contingency plans, you can prevent problems and solve them quickly and effectively. Medical professionals that have to make life-and-death decisions may have to respond to contingent events.[73]

Poor management is sometimes the cause of the problem, or responsible for not preventing or fixing the problem they created.[74] **BP** was criticized for not having an effective contingency plan in place after the oil rig in the Gulf of Mexico exploded. BP could have saved billions of dollars in fixing a disaster that could have been avoided in the first place, or at least minimized, with an effective contingency plan. The same is true of the **PG&E** fire crises.

When developing contingency plans, ask everyone involved what can go wrong and what should be done if it does go wrong. Also ask others within and outside the organization who have implemented similar plans. They may have encountered problems you haven't thought of, and they may have good contingency plans to suggest.

TIME MANAGEMENT

>> **LO 5.7:** Describe the value of a time log analysis.

Organizations pay people for their time, so time and attention are the most precious resources we have.[75] Ever heard that time is money? But because time is immaterial and we can't see it, time is valued cheaply.[76] If companies spent money as recklessly as they spend time, they'd be going out of business.[77]

Do you ever feel like there is never enough time? Or that you have so much to do but so little time? *Time management* refers to techniques that enable us to get more done in less time with better results. Time management (TM) skills will have a direct effect on your personal and career success.[78] We all have the same amount of time; the key is to learn to use it wisely,[79] and get the important things done.[80] That's what this section is all about.

Analyzing Time Use With a Time Log

The first step to successful time management requires using a time log, because most of us don't realize how we waste our time. A *time log* is a daily diary that tracks your activities and enables you to determine how you spend (and waste) your time each day. Exhibit 5-12 gives an example you can use as a template to develop your own time logs. You should keep track of your time every day over a period of one or two typical weeks. Try to keep the time log with you throughout the day. Fill in the Description column for each 15-minute time slot, if possible, describing what you did. How often do distractions and interruptions stop you from doing more important work?[81] If you are technically inclined, there are software programs for PCs and apps for smartphones that will track your time and use of these devices.

EXHIBIT 5-12

Time Management Tools

Daily Time Log

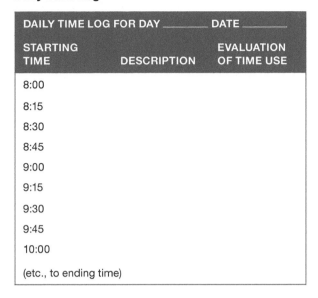

DAILY TIME LOG FOR DAY _____ DATE _____		
STARTING TIME	DESCRIPTION	EVALUATION OF TIME USE
8:00		
8:15		
8:30		
8:45		
9:00		
9:15		
9:30		
9:45		
10:00		
(etc., to ending time)		

Weekly Planner

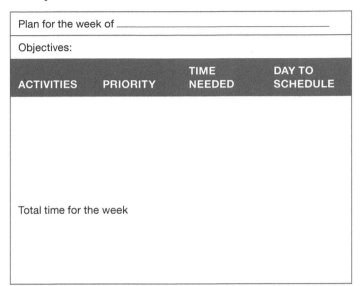

Plan for the week of _____

Objectives:

ACTIVITIES	PRIORITY	TIME NEEDED	DAY TO SCHEDULE

Total time for the week

Weekly Schedule

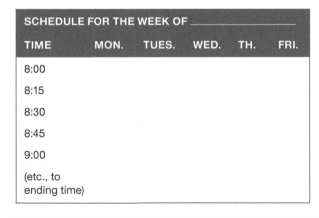

SCHEDULE FOR THE WEEK OF _____					
TIME	MON.	TUES.	WED.	TH.	FRI.
8:00					
8:15					
8:30					
8:45					
9:00					
(etc., to ending time)					

Daily Schedule

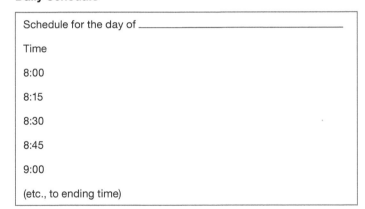

Schedule for the day of _____

Time
8:00
8:15
8:30
8:45
9:00
(etc., to ending time)

After completing your time logs, analyze the information and find time consumers you can eliminate. Write notes in the Evaluation of Time Use column of the log, using the following abbreviations:

- Determine how much time you are spending on your high-priority (HP) and low-priority (LP) responsibilities. How do you spend most of your time?

- Identify areas where you spend too much time (TT) and where you do not spend enough time (NT)

- Identify major interruptions (I) and distractions (D) like text, email, social media, and crisis situations (C) that keep you from doing what you want to get done. Our biggest time waster is often unnecessary interruptions. How can you eliminate them? We need blocks of uninterrupted time without distractions to be productive.[82] How about turning off all the electronic devices you don't need (and the noises they make) until you complete important tasks? Do you have effective contingency plans?

> **WORK APPLICATION 5-7**
>
> *Review your time log to identify your three biggest time wasters. How can you cut down or eliminate these time wasters?*

A Time Management System

Do you sometimes find yourself looking at your schedule and wondering when you'll find the time to do everything you need to do? If so, a time management system can help. The time management system is evidence-based (EBMgt) with a proven record of success and is used by thousands. First, we discuss priorities, followed by steps in the TM system. Try it.

Priorities

To meet your objectives, you need to know what tasks you need to get done to succeed and make them a priority. There usually isn't enough time to do everything, but there is time to do the most important things—priorities. TM is as much about what you don't do, as it is about what you do.[83] Why? Because things come up that distract and interrupt you from doing your priority tasks.[84]

Employees confessed to wasting about 40% of their time at work doing unimportant or downright irrelevant things.[85] Don't waste your time on social media and other things that keep you from completing your priorities.[86] Don't confuse being busy doing lots of activities with making progress on the important priorities. Focus on your most important priorities (which are often fewer than you think), doing them well, and eliminating essentially everything else. So assign a priority to each task, and do the most important thing first (without unnecessary interruptions)—make it a rule. Try to get as much uninterrupted time as you can every day so that you can meet your objectives.

Time Management Steps

The *time management system* involves the following three steps. Refer to Exhibit 5-12 for the template for each step.

> **Step 1. Plan each week.** Fill in a plan for the upcoming week using the "Weekly Planner" form. One caution: Planning too much is frustrating and causes stress when you cannot get everything done, so be realistic and focus on what you get done, not what is left to do that is less important anyway.
>
> **Step 2. Schedule each week.** Scheduling is key because it helps you avoid distractions and focus on your priorities, with minimal interruptions.[87] But you need to stay on your own schedules.[88] Start scheduling by filling in already-committed time slots, such as regular weekly meetings. Then schedule controllable events. Most managers should leave about 50% of the week unscheduled to accommodate unexpected events. Your job or schoolwork may require more or less unscheduled time.
>
> **Step 3. Schedule each day.** How you organize your day affects your productivity.[89] You need to focus on what you have to get done each day.[90] Start your day with your highest priority. Your schedule is in essence a to-do list. Leave your daily schedule flexible. Remember that if you are working on a high-priority item and you find yourself facing a lower-priority task, let it wait unless it is a true emergency. This will help you control interruptions and distractions.

To-Do Lists

The time management system described here works well for managers who have to plan for a variety of nonrecurring tasks. For managers and employees who deal primarily with routine tasks, a to-do list that prioritizes items may work quite well. The problem is that many people put too many items on their to-do list and focus on crossing things off; rather than prioritizing correctly and spending time doing important tasks.[91] We will discuss using a to-do list in Chapter 7. For now, realize that procrastination generally leads to more stress and can cause poor-quality work done late or at the last minute, as well as problems in relationships, jobs, finances, and health. So put the task on your to-do list and, as **Nike** says, "Just Do It!"

Forms similar to those in Exhibit 5-12 can be purchased in any number of formats, including in electronic forms such as your email, websites, and apps. Some are free, and some charge.

Time Management Techniques

One important thing we haven't mentioned yet is to respect others' time. Do your boss and coworkers waste your time making you wait to get your task done? Does your boss wait until the last minute to give you work with quick deadlines—and is it at the end of the day, or worse after hours? [92] The reason is often poor planning by bad bosses.[93] Do you waste other people's time?

Self-Assessment 5-2 contains 49 time management techniques arranged by management function. Planning and controlling are placed together because they are so closely related. Select and, more importantly, implement the items that will help you and others get more done in less time.

5-2 SELF-ASSESSMENT

Time Management Techniques

Following is a list of 49 ideas that can be used to improve your time management skills. Place a check mark in the appropriate box for each item.

Planning and Controlling Management Functions	1 = should do	2 = could do	3 = already doing	4 = doesn't apply to me
1. Use a time management system.	☐	☐	☐	☐
2. Use a to-do list and prioritize the items on it. Do the important things rather than the seemingly urgent things.	☐	☐	☐	☐
3. Get an early start on top-priority items.	☐	☐	☐	☐
4. Do only high-priority items during your best working hours (prime time); schedule unpleasant or difficult tasks during prime time.	☐	☐	☐	☐
5. Don't spend time performing unproductive activities to avoid or escape job-related anxiety. It doesn't really work; get the job done.	☐	☐	☐	☐
6. Throughout the day, ask yourself, "Should I be doing this now?"	☐	☐	☐	☐
7. Plan before you act.	☐	☐	☐	☐
8. Plan for recurring crises to eliminate crises (contingency planning).	☐	☐	☐	☐
9. Make decisions. It is better to make a wrong decision than to make none at all.	☐	☐	☐	☐

(Continued)

(Continued)

10. Schedule enough time to do the job right the first time. Don't be too optimistic about the amount of time it takes to do a job.	☐	☐	☐	☐
11. Schedule a quiet hour to be interrupted only by true emergencies. Have someone take messages or ask people who call then to call you back.	☐	☐	☐	☐
12. Establish a quiet time for the entire organization or department. The first hour of the day is usually the best time.	☐	☐	☐	☐
13. Schedule large blocks of uninterrupted (emergencies only) time for projects and so forth. If this doesn't work, hide somewhere.	☐	☐	☐	☐
14. Break large (long) projects into parts (periods).	☐	☐	☐	☐
15. Before abandoning a scheduled item to do something unscheduled, ask yourself, "Is the unscheduled event more important than the scheduled event?" If not, stay on schedule.	☐	☐	☐	☐
16. Do related activities (for example, making and returning calls, writing letters and memos) in the same time slot.	☐	☐	☐	☐
17. Schedule time for unanticipated events and let people know the time. Ask people to see or call you only during this time unless it's an emergency. Answer mail and do routine things while waiting for people to contact you. If people ask to see you— "Got a minute?"—ask whether it can wait until your scheduled time.	☐	☐	☐	☐
18. Set a scheduled time, agenda, and time limit for all visitors, and keep on topic.	☐	☐	☐	☐
19. Keep a clean, well-organized work area/desk.	☐	☐	☐	☐
20. Remove all non–work-related or distracting objects from your work area/desk.	☐	☐	☐	☐
21. Do one task at a time.	☐	☐	☐	☐
22. When paperwork requires a decision, make it at once; don't read through the paperwork again later and decide.	☐	☐	☐	☐
23. Keep files well arranged and labeled with an active and inactive file section. When you file an item, put a throwaway date on it.	☐	☐	☐	☐
24. Call rather than write or visit, when appropriate.	☐	☐	☐	☐
25. Delegate someone else to write letters, memos, and so forth.	☐	☐	☐	☐
26. Use form letters and form paragraphs in word-processing software.	☐	☐	☐	☐
27. Answer letters (memos) on the letter itself.	☐	☐	☐	☐
28. Have someone read and summarize things for you.	☐	☐	☐	☐
29. Divide reading requirements with others and share summaries.	☐	☐	☐	☐
30. Have calls screened to be sure the right person handles each call.	☐	☐	☐	☐

31. Plan before calling. Have an agenda and all necessary information ready; take notes on the agenda.	☐	☐	☐	☐
32. Ask people to call you back during your scheduled unexpected time. Ask about the best time to call them.	☐	☐	☐	☐
33. Have a specific objective or purpose for every meeting you conduct. If you cannot think of an objective, don't have the meeting.	☐	☐	☐	☐
34. Invite to meetings only the necessary participants, and keep them only as long as needed.	☐	☐	☐	☐
35. Always have an agenda for a meeting, and stick to it. Start and end as scheduled.	☐	☐	☐	☐
36. Set objectives for travel. List everyone you will meet with. Call the attendees or send them agendas, and have a file folder for each with all necessary data for your meeting.	☐	☐	☐	☐
37. Combine and modify activities to save time.	☐	☐	☐	☐
38. Set clear objectives for subordinates and make sure they know what they are accountable for; give them feedback and evaluate results often.	☐	☐	☐	☐
39. Don't waste others' time. Don't make subordinates wait idly for decisions, instructions, or materials, at meetings, and so on. Conversely, wait for a convenient time to speak to subordinates or others, rather than interrupting them and wasting their time.	☐	☐	☐	☐
40. Train your subordinates. Don't do their work for them.	☐	☐	☐	☐
41. Delegate activities in which you do not need to be personally involved, especially nonmanagement functions.	☐	☐	☐	☐
42. Set deadlines earlier than the actual deadline.	☐	☐	☐	☐
43. Use the input of your staff. Don't reinvent the wheel.	☐	☐	☐	☐
44. Teach time management skills to your subordinates.	☐	☐	☐	☐
45. Don't procrastinate; do it.	☐	☐	☐	☐
46. Don't be a perfectionist—define acceptable and stop there.	☐	☐	☐	☐
47. Learn to stay calm. Getting emotional only causes more problems.	☐	☐	☐	☐
48. Reduce socializing, but don't become antisocial.	☐	☐	☐	☐
49. Communicate well. Don't confuse employees.	☐	☐	☐	☐

IMPLEMENTING AND CONTROLLING STRATEGIES

>> LO 5-8: **Explain the importance of implementing and controlling strategies.**

The fifth and final step of the strategic planning process involves implementing and controlling strategies to ensure the mission and objectives, at all three levels, are achieved. Top managers are usually good at developing strategies, but strategy often fails at the implementation stage.[94] Here are some of the many reasons why strategies are not implemented. Recall that managers often make decisions (Chapter 4) but don't implement them.[95] Strategic plans often end up buried in bottom drawers; no action is taken to implement the strategy. Successful implementation of strategies requires having sufficient resources to achieve the objective, but top managers don't always provide the necessary resources.[96] Although it is important, it's not easy to get everyone aligned with the mission and to strive to meet the strategic objectives.[97] Corporate level strategy is developed by top level managers, but it has to go all the way down the organization to be implemented successfully.

Top and middle managers are more involved with the planning, whereas the lower-level functional managers and employees implement the operational strategies on a day-to-day basis. Successful implementation of strategies requires effective and efficient support systems throughout the organization to achieve the objective.[98] So you need to have the right people doing the right things—taking action to implement specific plans. Throughout Chapters 6 through 13, you will learn how to organize and lead so as to implement strategies.

As strategies are being implemented, they must also be controlled. *Controlling* is the process of monitoring progress and taking corrective action when needed to ensure that objectives are achieved (Chapter 1). To be implemented, strategy requires change, and people tend to resist change. You need to overcome the barriers that will try to prevent you from achieving your objectives. Another important part of controlling is staying within the budget when appropriate or changing it when necessary to meet changes in the dynamic environment. You will develop your change management skills in the next chapter and controlling skills in Chapters 14 and 15.

TRENDS AND ISSUES IN MANAGEMENT

Globalization, diversity, and integration of technology, as well as, ethics and social responsibility are integral to the success of businesses. Here we will examine the trends related to these topics.

Globalization and Diversity

As discussed in Chapters 2 and 3, with *globalization* and its *diversity*, business becomes more complex. MNCs like **P&G** doing business in more than 100 countries have to develop strategic plans in all the countries. With the wide diversity in the global village, MNCs must develop different strategies to appeal to the variety of cultures to meet local customs to satisfy customer needs. We also need to be culturally sensitive to ways we conceptualize, use, and control time in different countries.[99] Strategies today are global. **Citigroup** used a global retrenchment strategy as it sold or shut retail operations in more than half of 50 countries, reduced the number of U.S. branches by more than 62%, losing 69 million customers globally.[100]

Frenemies

The prior global strategic focus was to go it alone and compete head on. Today, the strategic trend is to be more collaborative with alliances.[101] Forming alliances (friends) with competitors (enemies) is called being *frenemies*. **Steve Jobs** and **Bill Gates** were among the first to be called frenemies, as **Microsoft** helped **Apple** develop operating systems and software. **Samsung** makes memory chips, displays, batteries and other components that go in rival Apple's iPhones,[102] Samsung will make $110 from each iPhone X Apple sells.[103] Auto makers are teaming up with tech companies to develop self-driving cars. Here are some of the companies working together: **Volkswagen** and **Aurora Innovation, BMW** and **Intel/Mobileye, Volvo** and **Uber,** and **Toyota** and Uber and **Lyft**.[104] Toyota will share a factory with **Mazda**, and foreign automakers will soon build more cars and trucks in America than **GM, Ford**, and **Fiat Chrysler**. Less than half (44%) of the U.S. sales are American made.[105]

Blue Ocean Strategy

W. Chan Kim and **Renée Mauborgne** developed the **Blue Ocean Strategy.** They are challenging current strategic management practices setting a trending shift to how we teach strategic management. The book has sold more than 3.6 million copies globally in 46 languages.

They developed red and blue oceans. *Red oceans* are all the industries in existence today; the known market space with cutthroat competition in existing industries. *Blue oceans* are all the industries not in existence today; the unknown market space unexplored and unpolluted by competition. So "'blue oceans' are vast, deep and powerful in terms of opportunity and growth."[106]

They teach how to find untapped demand to sell your product that makes the competition irrelevant by applying blue ocean concepts and tools in practice to create blue oceans. For more information visit https://www.blueoceanstrategy.com.

Technology

Technology is critical to competing in the global market as it provides analytical tools.[107] As technology changes, many businesses use the *imitation strategy* to stay competitive.[108] *Big data* is very important to focus strategies because it divides the total market into unique niche markets to better meet unique diverse customer needs. Companies using big data have greater quality and speed of executing their strategies because it helps in developing specific action plans to meet objectives.[109]

Goal Setting and Time Management

Recall that we focused on a low-tech time management system and, as stated, there is a lot of software and apps to help you manage your time. A few of the apps that will help you set goals and track your progress include the following: Keep Track of the Time You Spend Working Toward Your Goals: **ATracker**; Track Anything You Want, Any Way You Want: **Strides**; Track Both Good Habits and Bad Habits: **Way of Life**; Get Advanced Tracking and Visualization Tools: **GoalsOnTrack**; Use This Virtual Coach to Create Good Habits: **Coach.me**.[110] Here are some of the many time management apps: Use your time wisely: **Rescue Time**; Keep on top of all your tasks: **Remember The Milk**; Keep track of time spent on projects and tasks: **Toggl**; Boost motivation to complete tasks: **Focus Booster**.[111]

Global Crisis and Safety

Although technology creates great products, it can also fail and cause global crises. The **Boeing 737 Max 8** airplane in Indonesia and Ethiopia had two planes crash five months apart resulting in 346 dead. The crashes led to a near-global grounding of the planes to investigate the cause. This resulted in a major crisis for Boeing and the many airlines that use the planes because the 737 Max is a *cash cow* accounting for a third of the company's profits, and it lost sales and hurt its reputation for safety and also affects its stakeholders including its part suppliers.[112]

Ethics, CSR, and Sustainability

Although we didn't discuss *ethics* within the chapter topics, it is not an afterthought, as it fits better here, and we discussed the need to use ethical guides whenever you make decisions in Chapter 4. So while selecting strategies and planning, implementing, and controlling them, be sure to be ethical at all stages—maintain your moral standards. **Facebook** has been facing an ongoing

Companies that use big data may see the market more clearly, giving them an advantage over competitors.

crisis for over a year now since the **Cambridge Analytical** scandal. People question if Facebook is being *ethical* and *socially responsible* using peoples' data and the security of user data.[113]

Companies are adopting a strategic approach to *social responsibility (CSR)* to gain a competitive advantage and profits.[114] **Unilever** is making sustainable living commonplace. It has a *Sustainable Living Plan (USLP)* that is central to its business model. USLP sets out how Unilever is growing its business, while reducing its environmental footprint and increasing its positive social impact.[115] Part of ethics and CSR is being a good global corporate citizen. **FedEx**'s CSR plan includes giving $200 million to global communities by 2020.[116] Many MNCs are working on environmental *sustainability*. **Microsoft** will decrease its carbon emissions by 75% by 2030.[117]

$SAGE edge™

Want a better grade?

Get the tools you need to sharpen your study skills. Access practice quizzes, eFlashcards, video and multimedia, and more at **edge.sagepub.com/lussier9e.**

CHAPTER SUMMARY

Having read this chapter, you should understand the importance of effective planning and recognize the five planning dimensions and the differences between strategic and operational plans. You should understand the five steps in strategic planning and be able to develop a mission, analyze the environment, set effective objectives using a model, develop corporate-level and business-level strategies and operational-level plans, and implement and control strategies. You should understand operational strategies; know the four functional areas, the difference between standing and single-use plans, the use of contingency plans and crisis, and how to use a time management system; have techniques to improve your time management. A review of the learning objectives follows:

5-1.   Describe how strategic planning differs from operational planning.

The primary differences concern the time frame and the level of management involved. Strategic planning involves developing a mission and long-range objectives and plans; operational planning involves short-range objectives and plans. Upper-level managers develop strategic plans, and middle- and lower-level managers develop operational plans. The strategic planning process includes developing a mission, analyzing the environment, setting objectives, developing strategies (corporate, business, and functional levels), and implementing and controlling strategies.

5-2.   Explain the reason for conducting an industry, competitive, and company situation analysis.

The industry and competitive situation analysis is used to determine the attractiveness of an industry. It is primarily used at the corporate level to make decisions regarding which lines of business to enter and exit and how to allocate resources among lines of business.

The company situation analysis is used at the business level to determine the issues and problems that need to be addressed through the strategic planning process.

5-3.   State the criteria for an effectively written objective by identifying must and want criteria.

The parts of the objective are (1) *to* + (2) action verb + (3) singular, specific, and measurable result to be achieved + (4) target date. The must criteria need to be part of the objective and include being specific, measurable, and with a target date. The want criteria are desirable but not part of the objective and include being difficult but achievable, being participatively set, and having acceptance and commitment. When reading an objective, one can determine if the must criteria are met but not if the want criteria are met.

5-4.   Discuss corporate-level strategies in terms of the four grand strategies and the three growth strategies.

The four corporate-level strategies include growth, stability, turnaround, and retrenchment. With a *growth* strategy, the firm aggressively pursues increasing its size. With a *stability* strategy, the firm maintains the same size or grows slowly. With a *turnaround* strategy, the firm attempts a comeback; with *retrenchment*, it decreases in size. With a combination strategy, two or more of the three strategies are used for different lines of business.

The three growth strategies include concentration, integration, and diversification. With a *concentration* strategy, the firm grows aggressively in its existing line(s) of business. With *integration*, the firm grows by entering *forward* or *backward* line(s) of business. With *diversification*, the firm grows by adding *related* or *unrelated* products and/or services.

5-5. **Summarize the three business-level adaptive and competitive strategies.**

The three adaptive strategies are prospecting, defending, and analyzing and imitation. With the *prospecting* strategy, the firm aggressively offers new products or services and/or enters new markets. With the *defending* strategy, the firm stays with its product line and markets and aggressively tries to stop prospectors from taking its customers. With the *analyzing and imitation* strategy, the firm moves into new markets cautiously and/or offers a core product group and seeks new opportunities; analyzers commonly copy the successful strategies of prospectors. The three competitive strategies include differentiation, low cost, and focus. The *differentiation* strategy stresses developing a clear competitive advantage. The *low-cost* strategy stresses keeping prices low. The *focus* strategy targets a specific regional market, product line, or buyer group; it develops a niche to better meet the needs of its target customers than the mass marketers.

5-6. **Identify strategies for short-range operational planning.**

The four major *functional area strategies* include marketing, operations, finance, and human resources. *Standing plans* are policies, procedures, and rules developed for handling repetitive situations, whereas *single-use plans* are programs and budgets developed for handling one-time nonrepetitive situations.

5-7. **Describe the value of a time log analysis.**

The value of a time log is that it allows one to determine how time is wasted so that it can be eliminated or decreased to improve productivity.

5-8. **Explain the importance of implementing and controlling strategies.**

Strategies are of no value to the company unless it has plans stating how the objectives will be achieved, and a plan that is not implemented is also of no value. The implementation of the strategic plan must also be controlled to measure and monitor the progress of achieving the objective. Based on control, management must also not give up too soon and lose the benefits or get caught in the escalation of commitment and throw good money after bad.

REVIEW

Key Terms

acquisition, 162

adaptive strategies, 164

benchmarking, 155

business portfolio analysis, 162

competitive advantage, 155

contingency plans, 170

functional strategies, 167

grand strategy, 160

growth strategies, 161

management by objectives (MBO), 158

merger, 162

objectives, 156

operational planning, 150

policies, 168

procedure, 168

rules, 168

single-use plans, 169

situation analysis, 152

standing plans, 168

strategic planning, 150

strategy, 150

SWOT analysis, 153

Key Term Review

Complete each of the following statements using one of this chapter's key terms:

1. ____ is the process of developing a mission and long-range objectives and determining in advance how they will be accomplished.
2. ____ is the process of setting short-range objectives and determining in advance how they will be accomplished.
3. A ____ is a plan for pursuing a mission and achieving objectives.
4. A ____ focuses on those features in a company's environment that most directly affect its options and opportunities.

5. Through a____, the organization's internal environmental strengths and weaknesses and external environmental opportunities and threats are determined.

6. ____specifies how an organization offers unique customer value.

7. ____is the process of comparing the organization's products or services and processes with those of other companies.

8. ____state what is to be accomplished in specific and measurable terms with a target date.

9. ____is the process in which managers and their employees jointly set objectives for the employees, periodically evaluate performance, and reward according to the results.

10. ____is the overall corporate strategy of growth, stability, or turnaround and retrenchment, or for some combination of these.

11. ____include concentration, backward and forward integration, and related and unrelated diversification.

12. A____occurs when two companies form one corporation.

13. An____occurs when one business buys all or part of another business.

14. ____is the corporate process of determining which lines of business the corporation will be in and how it will allocate resources among them.

15. ____include prospecting, defending, and analyzing.

16. ____are developed and implemented by managers in marketing, operations, human resources, finance, and other departments.

17. ____are policies, procedures, and rules developed for handling repetitive situations.

18. ____provide general guidelines to be followed when making decisions.

19. A____is a sequence of actions to be followed in order to achieve an objective.

20. ____state exactly what should or should not be done.

21. ____are programs and budgets developed for handling nonrepetitive situations.

22. ____are alternative plans to be implemented if uncontrollable events occur.

Review Questions

1. What are the five planning dimensions?

2. What are the two types of plans?

3. Is there a difference between a plan and a strategy?

4. Which planning levels and their strategies are part of strategic planning?

5. What are the steps in the strategic planning process?

6. What is the relationship between the mission statement and developing strategies?

7. Why is a company situation analysis part of the strategic planning process?

8. What is the "writing effective objectives" model?

9. What criteria should an objective meet?

10. What are the grand strategies?

11. What is the difference between a merger and an acquisition?

12. What are the adaptive strategies?

13. What is the relationship between grand strategies and adaptive strategies?

14. What are the competitive strategies?

15. What are the common functional strategy areas?

16. What is the difference between standing plans and single-use plans?

17. Explain the use of a time log.

18. List and briefly describe the three steps in the time management system.

Communication Skills

The following critical-thinking questions can be used for class discussion and/or as written assignments to develop communication skills. Be sure to give complete explanations for all questions.

1. Why are strategic and operational planning important?
2. Should all businesses have corporate, business, and functional strategies?
3. Should a mission statement be customer focused?
4. Should all businesses formally analyze the environment?
5. Should all businesses have a competitive advantage?
6. Is it ethical to copy other companies' ideas through benchmarking?
7. Are both goals and objectives necessary for a business?
8. Is it important to write objectives?
9. As a manager, would you use management by objectives (MBO)?
10. Which growth strategy would you say is the most successful?
11. Why would a business use a focus strategy rather than trying to appeal to all customers?
12. Give examples of functional departments other than those mentioned in the text.

CASES

Case 5-1 Netflix, Inc.

Netflix, Inc. is the world's leading provider of Internet-based subscriptions for video streaming of TV series and movies with over 139 million subscribers. It was founded in 1997 by Reed Hastings and Marc Randolph with a focus on providing a wide range of movie rental options to consumers in the United States. Netflix's strategic objectives include:

- Offering in demand products and services
- Achieve high levels of customer convenience
- Expand its customer base and grow globally
- Develop original content

After the company was formed in 1997, it launched a DVD rental site in 1998 and a subscription service where customers could receive unlimited DVD rentals for a monthly fee in 1999. In 2007, the company achieved a key milestone as it launched its video streaming service that enabled customers to watch TV shows and movies on their personal computers. The company partnered with other consumer electronics firms to enable Netflix to be offered through videogame consoles such as the Xbox 360 and PS3 as well as Internet-connected devices such as the iPhone, iPad, and the Nintendo Wii. In 2010, the company made its first move to "go international" by offering its service in Canada. By 2016, Netflix was available in 190 countries around the world.

In 2013, Netflix launched its strategy to start developing original content with the release of "House of Cards." Since then the company has aggressively invested in more original content. By 2018, the company invested about $8 billion in developing original programming with plans to release 80 feature films and 700 new TV series. However in August 2017, Disney announced that it would be pulling its vast library of movies and TV shows from Netflix and other video streaming services. This new streaming service would go on to be called "Disney+" with a launch date of November 12, 2019.

In 2018, the company achieved strong business results including:

- **Earnings per share:** 30 cents
- **Revenue:** $4.19 billion
- **Domestic subscriber additions:** 1.53 million
- **International subscriber additions:** 7.31 million

Discussion Questions

1. How does Netflix engage in both strategic and operational planning?

2. Conduct a SWOT analysis of Netflix. Based on this analysis, what can you conclude about the company?

3. What is Netflix's competitive advantage?

4. What are the marketing functional strategies used at Netflix?

5. Do you really think it is beneficial for organizations to engage in a strategic planning process? Why or not?

6. Think about a student organization you have been involved with, or a part-time job, or internship you have held. Did this organization have a competitive advantage? If so, what was it?

References

https://media.netflix.com/en/about-netflix; https://netflixcompanyprofile.weebly.com; https://www.evolutionpartners.com.au/netflix-core-values-and-culture-statement-a-core-values-example.html; https://wp.nyu.edu/tonyfan/netflixs-strategy/; https://pestleanalysis.com/swot-analysis-of-netflix/; https://www.thrillist.com/entertainment/nation/disney-streaming-service-netflix-coming-soon; https://www.cnbc.com/2019/01/16/netflix-earnings-q4-2018.html; http://spotright.com/2018/08/07/netflix-marketing/

Case 5-2 The Not-So-Friendly Skies: Air Canada's Plan of Attack on U.S. Markets

Air Canada is Canada's largest airline and the largest provider of scheduled passenger services in the Canadian market, the Canada–U.S. transborder market, and the international market to and from Canada. In 2018, Air Canada together with its Air Canada Express regional partners carried more than 51 million passengers, offering direct passenger service to more than 220 destinations on six continents. Air Canada is a founding member of Star Alliance™, providing the world's most comprehensive air transportation network. Air Canada is among the 20 largest airlines in the world and employs 30,000 people. Its corporate headquarters are located in Montreal.

In 2019, the company will modernize its fleet by adding 45 Airbus A220-300 and take delivery of 18 Boeing 737 MAX. This builds on the airline's recent international fleet renewal of state-of-the-art and fuel-efficient Boeing 787 Dreamliners. Air Canada plans to operate 37 Boeing 787 Dreamliners by the end of 2019. (1)

For 2018, the company's financial results included the following:

- Operating income of $1.174 billion and EBITDAR (earnings before interest, taxes, depreciation, amortization, impairment, and aircraft rent, as a percentage of operating revenue) of $2.851 billion

- Record operating revenues of $18.065 billion

- Leverage ratio of 2.1 and record unrestricted liquidity of $5.725 billion

- Q4 operating income of $122 million and record Q4 EBITDAR of $543 million

In 2019, Air Canada is expanding its network with the announcement of new destinations including:

- Toronto to Vienna.

- Montreal to Bordeaux, Raleigh, North Carolina.

- Air Canada launched 29 new routes, including 11 new international routes:

   o Toronto to Shannon, Zagreb, Porto, Bucharest, Buenos Aires.

   o Montreal to Tokyo-Narita, Dublin, Bucharest, Lisbon.

   o Vancouver to Paris and Zurich.

Air Canada's financial targets for 2018-2020 are to achieve:

- Annual EBITDAR margin of 17–20%

- Annual ROIC of 13–16%

- Cumulative free cash flow of $2.0 billion to $3.0 billion

- Leverage ratio of 1.2 by the end of 2020

Air Canada has been pursuing a multifaceted growth strategy designed to generate revenue from new and existing sources and reduce personnel expenses. The company has been aggressively investing in technologies that enhance services to customers, including creating a Web-based reservation system and self-service check-in and adding entertainment systems to seatbacks and in-flight wireless Internet services (for a fee). It has also been bolstering its capacity to international destinations in the United States, Europe, and Asia. The airline also leverages its membership in the Star Alliance, which extends its network of destinations to 1,160 airports in 181 countries.

Air Canada serves about 220 destinations, primarily in Canada and the United States but also in the Asia/Pacific region and Europe. Together with regional affiliate Jazz, the carrier operates a fleet of about 330 aircraft from hubs in Calgary, Montreal, Toronto, and Vancouver. It extends its network as part of the Star Alliance global marketing group, which is led by United, Continental, and Lufthansa. (The alliance allows the airlines to sell tickets on one another's flights.) Besides its passenger business, Air Canada also hauls cargo and offers ground handling and travel arrangement services.(2)

With these powerful numbers as a backdrop, Air Canada is launching an all-out assault to the south. In May of 2017, the airline launches new service to a half dozen U.S. cities, including smaller markets such as Memphis and Savannah, Georgia. These will further expand a global route map that stretches from Algiers to Reykjavik and Taipei to Tel Aviv. The airline is also scouting Africa for future destinations.(3)

Every time an American flies on us they go "Oh my God, you're the best-kept secret. How did we not know about this?" That is what's music to my ears. [Ben Smith, Air Canada's president of passenger airlines.](4)

For Air Canada, this aggressive tactic comes with some hazards. Carriers like Delta Air Lines Inc. are notoriously sharp-elbowed when it comes to turf scuffles, and Emirates has the ability to throw on huge capacity as needed simply by moving the service to its superjumbo Airbus A380. In other words, Air Canada may be running a liability of being squeezed. The carrier is nowhere near the size of the American behemoths to the south, most of which do not take kindly to losing passengers to anyone. Long-haul flying typically commands higher fares and thus a more lucrative customer base, placing it among the more fiercely contested segments in air travel.(5)

I don't know when, but there will be a reaction by the U.S. carriers at some point when the supply of seats gets too high. In the short term, the U.S. carriers are probably focusing on some other markets as a group—Los Angeles, Orlando, San Francisco—but once they stop focusing on that, you might start to see some competitive response to Air Canada. For now, it is not on their radar screen. They have bigger fish to fry, such as the Middle East carriers. [Ben Smith, Air Canada's president of passenger airlines.](6)

If Warren Buffett, considered by many an investment guru, is any weather vane of corporate performance, bet on the U.S. industry firms winning the airlines war. Back in November of 2016, he or one of his portfolio managers (Ted Weschler and Todd Combs) heavily purchased three airline stocks: American Airlines, Delta Airlines, and United Continental Holdings Inc.(7)

Yet even if Air Canada wins this battle, it could lose the war. Industry analysts have noted that profitability comes hard to an industry in which price wars are rampant and customer loyalty a myth.

The airline industry has . . . very, very, very low incremental cost per seat with enormous fixed costs. The temptation to sell that last seat at a very low price is very high and sometimes it's very hard to distinguish between that seat and the last seat. It's labor-intensive and capital-intensive and largely [a] commodity-type business.(8)

That same Warren Buffett who invested in three U.S. airlines has traditionally detested airline stocks, famously saying in 2002, "If a capitalist had been present at Kitty Hawk back in the early 1900s, he should have shot Orville Wright."

Discussion Questions

1. Air Canada's launching new services to a half dozen U.S. cities could be categorized as what type of plan?

2. What environmental factors has Air Canada taken into account with its planned expansion into the United States? What might it have overlooked?

3. Which industry factors negatively affect the profitability of this industry?

4. Assume that Air Canada performed a SWOT analysis before it adopted the grand strategy of growth. What would have been the general results of that analysis to support growth?

5. Air Canada is expanding its operations. What actions has it taken to increase its core competencies in providing air services?

6. Air Canada has stated that it will launch new service to a half dozen U.S. cities, including smaller markets such as Memphis and Savannah. What is missing from these goals to make them effective objectives?

7. What specific growth strategy(ies) is Air Canada using?

Cumulative Case Questions

8. What type of resources would be needed to support Air Canada's expansion plans (Chapter 1)?

9. What international trade agreement(s) appear(s) to allow Air Canada to easily expand into the United States (Chapter 3)?

10. Decisions are made under conditions of either certainty, risk, or uncertainty. Which condition best describes Air Canada's decision to expand into the U.S. market (Chapter 4)?

References

(1) Air Canada Corporate Communications. (2017, February). Air Canada corporate profile. Retrieved from https://www.aircanada.com/content/aircanada/ca/en/aco/home/about/corporate-profile.html; (2) Gallo, R. (n.d.). Air Canada. Retrieved February 23, 2017, from http://0-subscriber.hoovers.com.liucat.lib.liu.edu/H/company360/fulldescription.html?companyId=157623000000000; (3) Bachman, J., & Domesco, F. (2017, February 15). Air Canada's plan of attack flies over America. *Bloomberg News*. Retrieved February 23, 2017, from http://montrealgazette.com/business/local-business/aerospace/air-canadas-plan-of-attack-flies-over-america; (4) Ibid.; (5) Ibid.; (6) Ibid.; (7) LaFon, H. (2016, November 14). Warren Buffett reports buying 3 airline stocks, cuts Walmart. Gurufocus.com. Retrieved February 23, 2017, from http://finance.yahoo.com/news/warren-buffett-reports-buying-airline-220611830.html; (8) Ibid.

SKILL BUILDER 5-1

Writing Objectives

For this exercise, you will first work at improving ineffective objectives. Then you will write nine objectives for yourself.

Objective

To develop your skill at writing objectives.

Skills

The primary skills developed through this exercise are:

1. *Management skill*—decision making (setting objectives is the first step to planning)

2. *AACSB competencies*—communication abilities, analytic skills, and application of knowledge.

3. *Management function*—planning (both strategic and operational)

Part 1

Indicate which of the "must" criteria each of the following objectives fails to meet and rewrite the objective so that it meets all those criteria. When writing objectives, use the following model:

To + action verb + specific and measurable result + target date

1. To improve our company image by the end of 2020
   Criteria not met:
   Improved objective:

2. To increase the number of customers by 10%
   Criteria not met:
   Improved objective:

3. To increase profits during 2020
   Criteria not met:
   Improved objective:

4. To sell 5% more hot dogs and soda at the baseball game on Sunday, June 14, 2021
   Criteria not met:
   Improved objective:

Part 2

Write three educational, three personal, and three career objectives you want to accomplish using Model 5-1, Objective Writing. Your objectives can be short term (something you want to accomplish today) or long term (something you want to have accomplished 20 years from now) or in between those extremes. Be sure your objectives meet the criteria for effective objectives.

Apply It

What did I learn from this experience? How will I use this knowledge in the future?

SKILL BUILDER 5-2

The Strategic Planning Process at Your College

This exercise enables you to apply the strategic planning process to your college or university as an individual and/or group.

Objective

To develop your planning skills.

Skills

The primary skills developed through this exercise are:

1. *Management skill*—decision making (conceptual, diagnostic, analytical, and critical thinking)
2. *AACSB competencies*—communication abilities, analytic skills, reflective thinking skills, and application of knowledge
3. *Management function*—planning (strategic)

Step 1. Developing the Mission

1. What is the mission statement of your university/college or school/department?
2. Is the mission statement easy to remember?
3. How would you improve the mission statement?

Step 2. Analyzing the Environment

1. Conduct a five-force competitive analysis, like that in Exhibit 5-4.
2. Complete a SWOT analysis, like that in Exhibit 5-6.
3. Determine the competitive advantage of your university/college or school/department.

Step 3. Setting Objectives

What are some goals and objectives of your university/college or school/department?

Step 4. Developing Strategies

1. Identify your university/college's or school/department's grand, adaptive, and competitive strategies.

_____

_____

2. Where would you place your program/major on the BCG growth-share matrix?

_____

_____

_____

_____

Step 5. Implementing and Controlling Strategies

How would you rate your university/college's or school/department's strategic planning? How could it be improved?

Apply It

What did I learn from this experience? How will I use this knowledge in the future?

SENDING MESSAGES

>> **LO 13-8:**   **Name the five steps in the process of sending face-to-face messages.**

Every time we talk, gesture, and write we are sending messages. An important part of a manager's job is to give instructions, which is sending a message. Have you ever heard a manager say, "This isn't what I asked for"? When this happens, it is usually the manager's fault. You must take 100% of the responsibility for ensuring that your messages are transmitted clearly. This section discusses the processes of planning and sending messages and how to properly check the receiver's understanding of the message.

Planning the Message

The vast majority of messages you send and receive in the workplace are quite simple and straightforward and need minimal planning, because they are routine. However, sometimes the message you need to transmit is difficult, unusual, or especially important. As noted earlier, for these kinds of messages, the richer the channel, the better. Before sending a message, answer these questions:

- **What?** What is the goal of the message? What specific action do you want to achieve? Careful with your word choice because words can be perceived in different ways.[96]
- **Who?** Determine who should receive the message.
- **How?** Plan how you will encode the message so that it will be understood. Select the appropriate words and channel(s) for the audience and situation. Have you ever heard "Sticks and stones will break my bones, but words will never hurt me"? Well, it's not true—derogatory words do hurt. This statement is used as a defensive response to hide the hurt caused by the words. So even if you believe society has gone overboard with political correctness, select your words carefully so you don't offend people and hurt relationships. Note that people have been forced to quit or retire for making derogatory comments, and business has been lost.
- **When?** When will the message be transmitted? Timing is important.
- **Where?** Decide where the message will be transmitted (setting).

The Message-Sending Process

As noted earlier, oral channels are richer than other channels, and face-to-face, oral communication is best when the message you must transmit is a difficult or complex one. When sending a face-to-face message, follow these steps in the **message-sending process** listed in Model 13-1. For step 1, start with small talk, then state your objective, transmit the details, be sure to check understanding, and, last, get a commitment to make sure the objective will be met and follow up to make sure it is.

Model 13-1 lists the five steps in the message-sending process.

message-sending process
A process that includes (1) developing rapport, (2) stating your communication objective, (3) transmitting your message, (4) checking the receiver's understanding, and (5) getting a commitment and following up.

WORK APPLICATION 13-5

Recall a specific task that a boss assigned to you. Identify which steps in the face-to-face message-sending process he or she did and did not use.

MODEL 13-1

The Message-Sending Process

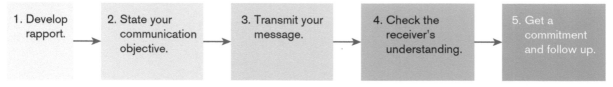

1. Develop rapport. → 2. State your communication objective. → 3. Transmit your message. → 4. Check the receiver's understanding. → 5. Get a commitment and follow up.

Checking Understanding: Feedback

feedback Information that verifies a message.

paraphrasing The process of restating a message in one's own words.

Feedback *is information that verifies a message.* It is an important management tool as it motivates and directs employee behavior.[97] The best way to get feedback is to ask for it.[98] Questioning, paraphrasing, and inviting comments and suggestions are all means of obtaining feedback that check understanding. Paraphrasing *is the process of restating a message in one's own words.* If the receiver of the message can answer the question or paraphrase the message, communication has taken place.

The Common Approach to Getting Feedback on Messages and Why It Doesn't Work

The most common approach to getting feedback is to send the entire message and then ask, "Do you have any questions?" Feedback usually does not follow because people tend not to ask questions, especially if they think they are dumb questions.[99]

After we send a message and ask if there are questions, we often make another common error. We assume we are good communicators and that if no one asks a question, the communication is complete—but this is often an illusion of mutual understanding.[100] In reality, recipients may have misunderstood the message. When this occurs, the result is often wasted time, materials, and effort.

How to Get Feedback on Messages

Use the following four guidelines when seeking feedback on messages.

- *Be open to feedback.* Effective feedback providers are open to listening to others and to changes. There are no dumb questions, so invite questions.[101] When someone asks a question, be responsive and patiently answer and explain things clearly. If people sense you get upset if they ask questions, they will not ask.

- *Be aware of nonverbal communication.* Make sure your nonverbal communication encourages feedback. For example, if you say, "I encourage questions" but you look at people as though they are stupid or you act impatient when they do ask, people will learn not to ask questions. You must also read nonverbal communication accurately. For example, if you are explaining a task to an employee and he or she has a puzzled expression, the employee is probably confused but may not be willing to say so. In such a case, you should stop and clarify things before going on.[102]

- *Ask questions.* You have to ask good questions to get good answers.[103] When you send messages, you should know whether recipients understand the messages before taking action. Direct questions about the specific information you have given will indicate if the receiver has been listening and whether he or she understands enough to give an appropriate reply. If the response is not accurate, you need to repeat the message, giving more examples or elaborating further.

- *Paraphrase.* The most accurate indicator of understanding is paraphrasing. Asking the receiver to paraphrase will affect his or her attitude. For example, saying, "Tell me what I just said so that I can be sure you will not make a mistake as usual" would probably result in defensive behavior or an error by the employee. Consider these examples of proper requests for paraphrasing:

"Now tell me what you are going to do so that we will be sure we are in agreement."

"Would you tell me what you are going to do so that I can be sure that I explained myself clearly?"

Notice that the second statement takes the pressure off the employee. The sender is asking for a check on his or her own ability, not that of the employee. These types of requests for paraphrasing should result in a positive attitude toward the message and the sender. They show concern for the employee and for communicating effectively.

Welcoming questions and asking questions will allow you to receive constructive feedback on messages you send.

©iStockphoto.com/skynesher

RECEIVING MESSAGES

>> **LO 13-9:** Identify and explain the three parts of the process of receiving messages and active listening.

The third step in the communication process requires the receiver to decode the message and decide if feedback is needed. This section discusses the process of receiving messages.

The Message-Receiving Process

The **message-receiving process** *includes listening, analyzing, and checking understanding.* The parts of the message-receiving process are illustrated in Model 13-2.

message-receiving process
A process that includes listening, analyzing, and checking understanding.

MODEL 13-2

The Message-Receiving Process

Listening	**Analyzing**	**Checking Understanding**
Pay attention	Think	Paraphrase
Avoid distractions	Wait to evaluate	Watch nonverbal behavior
Stay tuned in	until after listening	
(mentally paraphrase)		
Don't assume and interrupt		
Watch nonverbal behavior		
Ask questions		
Take notes (when appropriate)		
Convey understanding		

Listening

First you have to listen, as it is an important part of building trust and communications.[104] **Estée Lauder** president **Jane Lauder** says that leadership is about listening.[105] If we are asked, "Are you a good listener?" most of us would say yes. However, we are naturally poor listeners because we don't remember what was said.[106] To find out how good you are, complete Self-Assessment 13-1 to determine the level and the quality of your listening skills—be honest.

Note that in Model 13-2 under "Listening," there are eight tips to better listening. To implement the first three, shut off your phone and other distractions; concentration

---

13-1 SELF-ASSESSMENT

Listening Skills

For each statement, select the response that best describes how often you actually behave in the way described. Place the letter *A, U, F, O,* or *S* on the line before each statement.

A = almost always	U = usually	F = frequently	O = occasionally	S = seldom

_____ 1. I like to listen to people talk. I encourage others to talk by showing interest, smiling, nodding, and so forth.

_____ 2. I pay closer attention to people who are more similar to me than to people who are different from me.

_____ 3. I evaluate people's words and nonverbal communication ability as they talk.

_____ 4. I avoid distractions; if it's noisy, I suggest moving to a quiet spot.

_____ 5. When people interrupt me when I'm doing something, I put what I was doing out of my mind and give them my complete attention.

_____ 6. When people are talking, I allow them time to finish. I do not interrupt, anticipate what they are going to say, or jump to conclusions.

_____ 7. I tune people out who do not agree with my views.

_____ 8. While another person is talking or a professor is lecturing, my mind wanders to personal topics.

_____ 9. While another person is talking, I pay close attention to the nonverbal communication so I can fully understand what he or she is trying to communicate.

_____ 10. I tune out and pretend I understand when the topic is difficult for me to understand.

_____ 11. When another person is talking, I think about and prepare what I am going to say in reply.

_____ 12. When I think there is something missing from or contradictory in what someone says, I ask direct questions to get the person to explain the idea more fully.

_____ 13. When I don't understand something, I let the other person know I don't understand.

_____ 14. When listening to other people, I try to put myself in their position and see things from their perspective.

_____ 15. During conversations, I repeat back to the other person what has been said in my own words to be sure I understand what has been said.

If people you talk to regularly answered these questions about you, would they have the same responses that you selected? To find out, have friends fill out the questions using *you* (or your name) rather than *I.* Then compare answers.

To determine your score, give yourself 5 points for each *A,* 4 for each *U,* 3 for each *F,* 2 for each *O,* and 1 for each *S* for statements 1, 4, 5, 6, 9, 12, 13, 14, and 15. For items 2, 3, 7, 8, 10, and 11, the scores reverse: 5 points for each *S,* 4 for each *O,* 3 for each *F,* 2 for each *U,* and 1 for each *A.* Write the number of points on the lines next to the response letters. Now add your total number of points. Your score should be between 15 and 75. Note where your score falls on the continuum below. Generally, the higher your score, the better your listening skills.

15	20	25	30	35	40	45	50	55	60	65	70	75

Poor listener   Good listener

is key. Ever hear the advice that we should "listen more and talk less"? Former **Assurant** CEO **Robert Pollock** says you learn more when your mouth is closed and your ears are open.[107] Everyone knows something that you don't know, so listen and learn. We'll discuss active listening shortly.

Analyzing

Analyzing is the process of thinking about, decoding, and evaluating the message. As the speaker sends the message, you should be doing two things:

- *Thinking.* Use the speed of your brain positively by mentally repeating or paraphrasing, organizing, summarizing, reviewing, and interpreting what is being said often.

- *Waiting to evaluate until after listening.* You should first listen to the entire message without perception bias (Chapter 10), and then come to your conclusions.

Checking Understanding

Checking understanding is the process of giving feedback. After you have listened to the message (or while listening if it's a long message), check your understanding of the message by doing two things:

- *Paraphrasing/questioning.* Give feedback by paraphrasing the message back to the sender, and ask questions if you don't understand something.

- *Watching nonverbal behavior.* As you speak, watch the other person's nonverbal communication. If the person does not seem to understand what you are talking about, clarify the message before finishing the conversation.

Do you talk more than you listen? Ask your boss, coworkers, or friends, who will give you an honest answer. Regardless of how much you listen, if you follow the guidelines discussed in this section, you will become a better listener. Review items 1, 4, 5, 6, 9, 12, 13, 14, and 15 in Self-Assessment 13-1, which are the statements that describe good listening skills. Effective listening requires responding to the message to ensure mutual understanding.

Retentive Listening

Hearing what people are saying is nice, but it's not enough. *Retentive listening* is not just about hearing what is said, which most of us can do; it's really about remembering the message, which takes concentration. How's your memory, are you *mindful*?[108] Business communications usually require taking appropriate action based on the message. How can we take action if we don't understand or remember the message? Can you see how multitasking kills concentration and memory?[109] Refer back to mindfulness to develop your retentive listening skills.

WORK APPLICATION 13-6

Refer to Self-Assessment 13-1. What is your weakest listening skill? Give an example of how your listening skills have had an impact on you at work.

Active Listening

As you know, the message-receiving process is not a simple linear process. We listen, analyze, and check understanding constantly as we have a conversation, as well as change from receiver to sender of messages. So the best way to receive messages is to be an active listener. *Active listening* puts the three parts of the message-receiving process together by using verbal and nonverbal communications to show the sender that the receiver is fully engaged and cares about the sender as a person.[110] Thus, it fosters good human relationships.

Active listeners follow the eight guidelines of listening listed in Model 13-2. Here is a little more detail. Active listeners look for signs that the other person wants to talk; they ask open-ended questions like "How is it going?" and encourage the person to elaborate. They lean forward and nod their head, look at the person and make eye contact, and ask questions and paraphrase to ensure they understand what the person is saying and means. Active listeners use reflective responses, showing empathic concern,[111] which are discussed in the next section.

RESPONDING TO MESSAGES

>> LO 13-10:   **Define five response styles.**

The fourth and last step in the communication process is responding to the message. However, not all messages require a response, but with oral communication, the sender often expects a response.

As a sender transmits a message, how we respond directly affects the communication progression. Our comments can encourage or cut off the conversation, and they can help the sender keep calm or get emotional. But before you learn about the five response styles, complete Self-Assessment 13-2 to determine your preferred response style.

13-2 SELF-ASSESSMENT

Your Preferred Response Style

Select the response you would actually make as the supervisor in the five situations that follow:

1. "I can't work with Paul. He is always complaining about me and everyone else, including you, boss. Why does he have to be my partner on this assignment? We can't work together. You have to assign someone else to be my partner."

   A. "I'm sure there are things that you do that bother Paul. You'll have to work things out with him."

   B. "What has he said about me?"

   C. "Can you give me some examples of the specific things that he does that bother you?"

   D. "I'll talk to Paul. I'm sure we can improve or change the situation."

   E. "So Paul is really getting to you."

2. "We can't make the deadline on the Procter Project without more help. We've been having some problems. A major problem is that Connor and Lily are recent college grads, and you know they don't know anything. I end up doing all the work for them. Without another experienced person, my team will not get the job done on time."

   A. "Tell me more about these problems you are having."

   B. "Did you see the game last night?"

   C. "You are really concerned about this project, aren't you?"

   D. "You will have to stop doing the work and train the new people. They will come through for you if you give them a chance."

   E. "Don't worry. You're a great project leader. I'm sure you will get the job done."

3. "Congratulations on being promoted to supervisor. I am wondering what to expect. After all, we go back five years as good friends in this department. It will seem strange to have you as my boss."

   A. "Things will work out fine; you'll see."

   B. "I take it that you don't like to see things change. Is that what you mean?"

   C. "Just do a good job, and there will not be any problems between us."

   D. "Is Chris feeling any better?"

   E. "Tell me how you think things will change."

4. I wish you would do something about Gloria. She is always wearing short, tight clothes to work. I think the way she dresses is inappropriate for the office."

   A. "So you think this situation is indecent, is that it?"

   B. "I can't tell Gloria how to dress. Why don't you turn your desk so you don't notice."

C. "Don't let it bother you. I'm sure it's fine."

D. "What do you think I should do?"

E. "Are you feeling well today?"

5. "I can't take it anymore. I've been running around like a fool waiting on all these customers, but all they do is yell at me and complain."

A. "Are you going to the party tonight?"

B. "What is the most irritating thing the customers are doing?"

C. "With Erin being out today, it's been crazy. But tomorrow she should be back and things

should be back to normal. Hang in there; you can handle it."

D. "The customers are really getting to you today, hey?"

E. "I told you during the job interview that this is how it is. You have to learn to ignore the comments."

To determine your preferred response style, in the following table circle the letter you selected in situations 1 to 5. The column headings indicate the style you selected.

	ADVISING	DIVERTING	PROBING	REASSURING	REFLECTING
1	A	B	C	D	E
2	D	B	A	E	C
3	C	D	E	A	B
4	B	E	D	C	A
5	E	A	B	C	D
Total	_____	_____	_____	_____	_____

Add up the number of circled responses per column. The total for all columns should equal 5. The column with the highest number represents your preferred response style. The more evenly distributed the numbers are among the styles, the more flexible you are at responding.

Response Styles

Five typical response styles are shown in Exhibit 13-7 along with stating when they are appropriate for the situation. We will present the five response styles using an example of each response style being given. Suppose an employee voices the following complaint to you as a supervisor:

"You supervise me so closely that you disrupt my ability to do my job."

"We will consider how you as a manager might respond to this complaint using each response style."

Advising

Advising responses provide evaluation, personal opinion, direction, or instructions and are often confrontational; it is helpful in solving problems.[112] Advising tends to close or limit discussion or direct the flow of communication away from the sender to the receiver. Being quick to give advice may stop people from discussing what is really on their mind, and they may not even need or want your advice. So it is best to only give advice when asked for it. But rather than simply telling people what to do, help them figure out their own solution to problems. Say something like, what do you think is a good solution, or what action are you thinking about taking?

A manager's advising response to the employee's complaint might be "You need my directions to do a good job, since you lack experience" or "I disagree. You need my instructions, and I need to check your work." Note that in this situation, the employee did not ask for advice, but it was given anyway.

EXHIBIT 13-7

Five Typical Response Styles

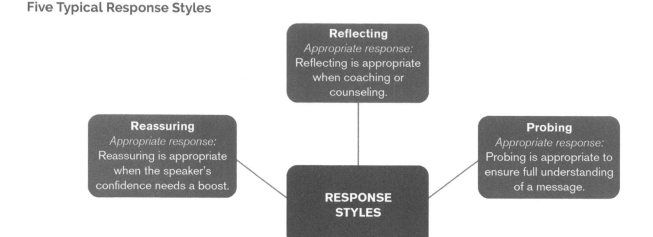

Diverting

Diverting responses switch the focus of the communication to a new message—in other words, they change the subject. Like advising, diverting tends to redirect, close, or limit the flow of communication. People usually want to be heard,[113] and diverting responses used during the early stages of receiving the message may cause the sender to feel that the message is not worth discussing or that the other party's message is more important. But there are times when it is best to change the subject to avoid conflict.

A manager's diverting response might be "You've reminded me of a manager I once had who . . ."

Probing

Probing responses ask the speaker to give more information about some aspect of the message. Probing can be useful when you need to get a better understanding of the situation. Effective managers ask good questions for clarity to ensure they understand the message. When probing, "What?" questions are preferable to "Why?" questions. After probing, responses in other styles are often needed.

A manager's probing response might be "What do I do to cause you to say this?" Note that "Why do you feel this way?" is *not* an appropriate probing response.

Reassuring

Reassuring responses are given to reduce the intensity of the emotions and give confidence associated with the message. Essentially you're saying, "Don't worry; everything will be OK" or "You can do it."

A manager's reassuring response might be "Don't worry, I will not be supervising you so closely for much longer" or "Your work is improving, so I may be able to provide less direction soon."

Reflecting

Reflecting responses *paraphrase the message and communicate understanding and acceptance to the sender.* When reflecting, be sure *not* to use the sender's exact words, or the person may feel you are mimicking. Reflecting in your own words often leads to the most effective communication and the best human relations because it confirms that you are interested in listening to them and that you value them as a person. As the communication progresses, it may be appropriate to change to other response styles. However, sometimes people just want empathic concern,[114] someone to listen to what is going on with them—not give them advice, solve their problem, or talk about the other person.

A manager's reflecting response might be "My checking up on you annoys you?" or "You don't think I need to check up on you—is this what you mean?" Note that these responses allow the employee to express feelings and to direct the communication.

reflecting responses
Responses that paraphrase a message and communicate understanding and acceptance to the sender.

WORK APPLICATION 13-7

Recall two oral messages you received and your responses to them. Identify your response style, and give examples of responses you might have given using two other response styles.

13-4 APPLYING THE CONCEPT

Response Styles

Identify the response style exemplified in each statement in the following two situations.

A. advising

B. diverting

C. probing

D. reassuring

E. reflecting

Betty Sue: Katniss, Do you have a minute to talk?

Katniss: Sure what's on your mind?

Betty Sue: Being the AD [athletic director], you know that I use the weight room after the football team. Well, my track team has to return the plates to the racks, put the dumbbells back, and so forth. I don't get paid to pick up after the football team. After all, they have the use of the room longer than we do. I've complained to Usain [the football coach], but all he says is that's the way he finds it, or that he'll try to get the team to do a better job. But nothing happens.

Katniss responds:

_____ 26. "I want you to go and work it out with Usain."

_____ 27. "Thanks for telling me about it; I'll talk to Usain to see what's going on."

_____ 28. "I almost forget to tell you, congratulations on beating UNH."

_____ 29. "So you don't think it's fair for you and your team to pick up after the football team."

_____ 30. "How long have you been picking up after the football team?"

Administrative
Assistant: Carl, do you have a minute to talk?

Boss: Sure, what's up, Mary?

AA: Are you aware of all the swearing people do in the operations department? It carries through these thin walls into my work area. It's disgusting.

Boss:

_____ 31. "So you don't like swearing—is that it?"

_____ 32. "What specific swears are they saying that you find offensive?"

_____ 33. "No. I didn't know because I don't spend much time in the ops department. But I'll look into it."

_____ 34. "Just ignore the swearing. Don't let it bother you."

_____ 35. "Are you going to the company picnic?"

_____ 36. "Why don't you talk to them about it?"

_____ 37. "It seems like you find swearing offensive."

CRITICISM

>> **LO 13-12:** **Discuss guides to giving and receiving criticism.**

Communication affects performance, and feedback is used to improve performance, and getting and giving feedback in the form of criticism can lead to emotional responses. So we want to give and receive criticism using emotional intelligence (EI). Regardless of the role you are in, there are ways to give and receive criticism effectively. That's what this section is all about.

Giving Criticism

An important part of leadership is to provide constructive criticism by giving feedback on things that can be improved and issues that can be avoided. Firms, including hedge fund **Bridgewater**, developed a "culture of candor" that encourages criticism to improve everyone's performance.[145] Feedback is best received when rooted in good intentions and given with empathy in the spirit of helping others and coming from a person who is trusted and respected.[146] So never put the person down using words like *never* and *always* and saying "You're doing it wrong" ("You're wrong") or "You don't know what you're doing/talking about." Criticism should not be about the person, and it must be something the person can actually change. It should have two parts.

1. Criticism should state the *specific* behavior that can be improved.
2. It should *specify* the improved behavior (which may need to be taught).

Chapter 14's section on coaching will provide more details on how to accomplish this task.

Getting the Person to Ask for Criticism

By far the best way to give criticism is to get others to ask for it. Show genuine concern for them. Here's how. Don't say, "You're doing that wrong. Let me show you how to. . . ." Do say, "Would you like me to show you a way to do that task faster and easier?" How would you respond to each of these statements?

Criticizing the Boss

Criticism that moves upward is a different matter. Even when bosses ask, they usually don't want to hear personal criticism.[147] If your boss asks you in a meeting for feedback on how good a manager he or she is or how he or she can improve, it may sound like the ideal opportunity to unload your complaints—but in such a situation, the first rule of thumb is to never publicly criticize anyone, especially your boss, even if specifically asked to do so. You are better off airing criticism to your boss in private and only if you know he or she really wants to hear it, will accept it, and will actually change behaviors. Don't criticize your boss behind his or her back, either; bosses often find out about it. Again, venting isn't good for us.

Getting Criticism

While praise is great to motivate repeat performance, it doesn't usually actually improve our performance. Criticism is not something we look forward to, but getting feedback in the form of criticism is necessary if we want to see continuous improvement.[148] Criticism from your boss, peers, or employees is painful—the truth can hurt. People do not really enjoy being criticized, even when it is constructive. Do you handle it poorly? How good are you at accepting criticism and changing to improve? However, it is important to keep three things in mind:

- More often than not, your boss and others want to help you succeed—they are helping you improve.

- Don't take it personally. It's not really about you as a person, it's about a specific behavior you can change to improve. Let's admit it—we can all improve—through criticism. Even if you disagree, there is usually some truth about your performance that you can improve. Psychologist **Michael Woodward** says, "Look for the nugget of value."[149]

- Keep the phrase "no pain, no gain" in mind when it comes to criticism. If you want to improve your chances of having a successful career, seek honest feedback and use it to improve your performance.

Performance appraisals are a formal system of giving criticism; refer to Chapter 9 for tips on accepting criticism under the heading "Being Evaluated" (page 331). Finding out what your boss really thinks about your performance can be scary, but it is the best way to find out how to improve your performance that will lead to the highest performance reviews, raises, and promotions.

Let go of ego-defensive behavior. When you get criticism from anyone, whether you ask for it or not, view it as an opportunity to improve, stay calm (even when the other person is emotional), and don't get defensive, deny something you did, or blame others.[150] This behavior is used by people to avoid having to change their behavior to improve[151]—its them not me—ever seen it? If you do (and it is hard not to when you feel attacked), the person will stop giving feedback, and you will not improve your performance. Apologies help, but you need to change to improve.[152]

Recall from Chapter 10 that **Apple**'s **Steve Jobs** could get very emotional and yell negative personal criticisms when he wasn't getting his way but that **Microsoft**'s **Bill Gates** was very successful in negotiating with Jobs because he didn't yell insults back. Gates stayed calm, spoke softly, and calmed Jobs down and then continued focusing on conducting business; this is how he closed multiple beneficial company deals between the two *frenemies*.

WORK APPLICATION 13-9

How would you rate yourself on your ability to accept criticism without getting emotional and defensive? How could you improve your ability to accept criticism?

TRENDS AND ISSUES IN MANAGEMENT

Globalization, diversity, and integration of technology, as well as, ethics and social responsibility are integral to the success of businesses. Here we will examine the trends related to these topics.

Globalization and Diversity

Information technology has been a major factor in the globalization of business. However, language and cultural differences make it challenging to conduct business globally. In general, there is no difference in culture and gender communications ability.

But there are *cultural* differences in the acceptance of displaying emotions at work. For example, in countries with greater freedom of expression and social resources (including Chile, Sweden, and the United States), showing emotions is more acceptable than in other countries (including Ghana, Nigeria, and Nepal).

U.S. women tend to be more sensitive to criticism than men, and women are more likely than men to express their feelings. Organizations have emotional cultures (norms of sharing and suppressing specific emotions). Industries dominated by men, such as police officers and firefighters, tend to have macho cultural norms of suppressing emotions and use peer pressure to discourage behavior such as admitting and discussing mental stress from the job.[153]

Companies with more women in leadership positions perform better. Is the difference due to men and women communicating differently verbally and nonverbally? Of course, we are talking in general terms, knowing there are exceptions.[154] Female leaders are more likely to try for collaboration, treating others as equals and checking in frequently. Women aren't "girls," and many resent this negative stereotype. Younger workers tend to lack communication skills, especially writing skills. There is also debate regarding millennials spending too much time on social media and texting, making their face-to-face communications less effective than those of older workers.[155] Recall the importance of emotions and empathy at work. Well, millennials want it, but they display far less empathy than older generations.[156]

Technology

Digital technology is changing how we conduct business. How many of your purchases are online? While **Bank of America** and **JPMorgan Chase** spent years following a growth strategy by acquiring smaller banks for more branches, **Citigroup** strategically focused on building its digital infrastructure forecasting that consumers are ready to leave branches for digital transactions. Today, Bank of America and JPMorgan are ramping up digital banking but, unlike Citigroup, they are both operating more than 4,000 expensive branches.[157]

Algorithms read nonverbal cues better than you can—welcome to the age of AI driven empathy. **Cogito** is a real-time app that helps call center employees read and respond better to emotions to improve handling complaints in less time with better results.[158] There is new software using algorithms to change the conversation—literally. One new program runs like a spell check for empathy to improve your emails to ensure your intentions will be properly understood to help you develop and maintain good relationships.[159] Believe it or not, with extreme doubt this will succeed, **Facebook** is spending millions on research to message your friends telepathically (essentially just thinking about it).[160]

Ethics and CSR

It can be tempting to lie during communications. One expert estimates that we are lied to as many as 200 times per day. Lying is harder for us to do in person than it is in writing. Ever got a message saying, I'm late because. . . . or I didn't get your text/email? and wonder if it's true? Nonverbal communication in person can give us clues that we are being lied too. When people are not writing or talking like they usually do using different nonverbal body language (not looking at you or making eye contact, gestures, vocal quality, posture) and they are being very vague, they may be lying to you. In writing, people tend to write differently when they lie, as they tend to be vague (intentionally lead you to a wrong conclusion rather than directly lie), don't use pronouns (avoid ownership of lie), and change tense (lying in the present about a past event). But some people lie so much that it's hard to tell when they are lying.[161]

With the growing use of *social media*, many companies are developing policies for their use at work, and monitoring employees' use of it, including **Apple**, **CNN**, **Cisco**, and **Coca-Cola**. Social media is also used in strategic planning, as **Facebook** helps analyze the past, **Twitter** helps understand the present, and **Pinterest** helps identify what customers might do or buy in the future to aid in developing strategic plans.[162] Unfortunately, a tweet or a Facebook post has the potential to be ethically problematic and bring bad press to be more socially responsible.

Appendix: Career Management and Networking

Learning Objectives

After studying this appendix, you should be able to:

A-1. List the five steps in career planning. **PAGE 349**

A-2. Identify the five steps in the networking process. **PAGE 355**

A-3. Describe a one-minute self-sell and its three parts. **PAGE 355**

This appendix was revised by Erica Berte, associate professor of management, College of Management, Metropolitan State University, Saint Paul, Minnesota.

CAREER MANAGEMENT

>> LO A-1: List the five steps in career planning.

Career success is probably on your mind, as it is important to both work and life satisfaction. A *career* is a sequence of related job positions, involving increasing responsibility and increased compensation and held over a lifetime. Career success depends on hard work and planning. Remember you must take the responsibility for managing your career; you can't simply rely on others to give you jobs, raises, and promotions. This appendix will help you with your career by discussing career planning and development and getting a job. If you have not completed Self-Assessment 9-1, "Career Development," in Chapter 9, do so now (see page 324).

©iStockphoto.com/jeffbergen

Career Planning and Development

There is a difference between career planning and career development. **Career planning** *is the process of setting career objectives and determining how to accomplish them.* **Career development** *is the process of gaining skill, experience, and education to achieve career objectives.*

career planning The process of setting career objectives and determining how to accomplish them.

career development The process of gaining skill, experience, and education to achieve career objectives.

Most colleges offer career-planning services that can help you. The career-planning counselor's role is not to find you a job but to help you set realistic career objectives and plans. The steps in the *career-planning model* that follow can help you develop your own career plan. Skill Builder A-1 will guide you in the use of these steps to develop your own career plan.

Step 1. Self-assessment. Who are you? What are your interests, values, needs, skills, experience, and competencies? What do you want to do during your career? The key to career success is to determine what you do well, what you enjoy doing, and how to find a job that combines your interests and skills. If you aren't sure what your interests are, your college career center may have a test to help match you with a job. You can also take a test online at some websites.

Step 2. Career preferences. Others can help you get a job, but you are responsible for selecting your career. Based on your self-assessment, you must decide what you want from your job and career and prioritize these preferences. What motivates you?

Some of the things you should consider as you think about your career preferences are (1) what industry you want to work in, (2) what size organization you want to work for, (3) what type of job(s) you want in your career and which functional areas interest you (production/operations, marketing, finance, human resources, and so on), (4) what city, state, or country you want to work in, and (5) how much income you expect when you start your career and five years and 10 years after that.

Once you have thought about these preferences, read about the career areas that interest you. Talk to people in your school's career-planning office and to people who hold the types of jobs you are interested in. (This is called networking, and we discuss networking in more detail later in this appendix.) Determine the requirements and qualifications you need to get a job in the career that interests you. If you are not 100% sure of the career path you want to consider this is not a problem. You can choose a few areas and experiment by participating in an internship, getting involved in research with one of your professors, or taking on a part-time job and/or summer job. These experiences could assist you in having a better idea of the types of jobs you would perform in a particular career path and also help you to build your résumé improving your chances to land the job you want after graduation.

Step 3. Career objectives. You need to set goals and act on them. Set short- and long-range objectives, using the planning guidelines discussed in Chapter 5.

Step 4. Plan. Develop a plan that will enable you to attain your objectives. This is where career development fits in. First, you must determine what skills, education, and experiences, you need in order to progress from your current level to the next level and beyond in order to achieve your career goals. Second, you need to identify where and how you are going to acquire these new skills, education, and experiences. Third, build a detailed plan establishing clear goals that you need to achieve for a successful career. Consider what financial resources you will need, the length of this process, and what steps you need to accomplish first. At the same time, remember that a plan must be flexible to be open to taking advantage of unplanned opportunities.

Step 5. Control. Review your objectives, check your progress at least every few months, and change and develop new objectives and plans. Update your résumé as you improve your skills and experience. Having a good career coach or mentors can help you get a job and advance through career stages. A coach or mentor can be anyone more experienced than you in a certain field that can talk with you about their own career path, and how they achieved it. Identify people that can guide you and invite them for a coffee and openly ask for career advice. You will be surprised by how successful people enjoy talking about the journey they took to be where they are. There is a big chance they had several mentors in their life and they would be glad to mentor others too.

WORK APPLICATION A-1

What career development efforts are you making?

Getting a Job

Based on your career plan, you prepare a résumé and cover letter for each job, research the organization, and prepare for the interview. But let's start with some pre-job search considerations.

Pre-Job Search Considerations

These ideas can help you.

- **Search Yourself.** Many employers will look you up on the Internet researching online to verify what they can find about you, and forming an opinion about who you are even before talking to you. Therefore before you start looking for a job, research your online presence and take down any unprofessional photos, posts, or comments. Be mindful in any social media input you give. Employers can easily access everything available online. This search of your presence online can happen at any moment, so even after being hired be careful of how you conduct yourself on the online environment.

- **Phone Message.** You may also get calls from employers, so make sure your phone messages are business-like and sound professional; for example, skip the music.

- **Organization and Job Selection.** Make sure you go online and search the values and the culture of the organization you are applying to for a job. Check for fit with your own values. If you believe that preserving the environment is important don't apply for a job in an organization that is known for damaging the environment. In addition, get a job in a field that will add the experience you need to progress in the career path you want to follow. Avoid taking any job just to have a job, because your experience can move you in a direction you don't want and this can eventually hurt your chances of getting into your chosen career.

- **Jobs While Searching.** If you are thinking, "Well, I need money," here are three options to help get you to the job you really want. (1) Work for a temporary agency. This can give you some experience and get you into some organizations you may want to work for that could lead to networking and a full-time job. Agency staff commonly help improve résumés. (2) Be a substitute teacher. In most states, you don't need to be a certified teacher, and in some states, you don't even need to have completed your college degree. Temping and subbing can be tough, but you can earn money. You can also easily take days off from temping, and when subbing, you are done with work early enough to get to job interviews as you search for the job in your field that you really want to progress to in your career. (3) If you know you want to work for a specific organization, do an internship or take an entry-level job to get your foot into the door. If you do a good job, you may be able to move up through a promotion from within to the job you really want.

- **Target Your Search Using Keywords.** Don't simply send out hundreds of generic résumés. Select jobs you want and customize your résumé and cover letter to match the job. In the objective, state the company name and title of the job you want. Most large companies scan résumés for keywords. To increase your chances of being in the interview pile, you need to carefully read the job description and use the exact words in your résumé, and don't vary the terms for variety. After selecting the targeted job, your entire résumé should focus on letting the employer know you can do the job.

Résumé and Cover Letter

Your résumé and the cover letter you send with it are your introduction to the organization you wish to work for. If the résumé is messy or contains mistakes, you may not get an interview. The cover letter should be short—one page or less. Its purpose is to introduce your résumé and to request an interview. Not all job applications will require a cover letter, but in case they do you need to know how to develop one. The résumé should also be short; one page is recommended, unless you have extensive education and experience. Exhibit A provides a sample résumé. Go online and search for other résumés in the area you want to work for. This will give you an idea of common terminology used to describe job experience and also the different formats you can use. Note that the objective lists a specific job and company, so again target your search by listing the job and the company for each and every job you apply for. Skill Builder A-2 will give you practice in preparing a résumé.

- *Format.* Your résumé makes the first impression an employer has about you. The information it presents should be clear and well organized. Divide the content by headings, present the information in a chronological way, and take advantage of tools like bullets. Arial and Times New Roman theme fonts, as well as 12-point font, are very commonly used. You may want to show your personality and use some creativity in your résumé, depending on the job you are applying for (if it requires creativity), but this can be risky.

- *Accomplishments.* When listing internships and other work experience, volunteer work, and sports on your résumé, be sure to focus on accomplishments and skills that can be used on the job you are applying for. Common desirable job skills employees look for are: communication, leadership, creativity, teamwork, as well as analytical and problem solving. When possible use your experiences to inform that you developed these skills.

- *Transferable Skills.* When you are applying for a professional job unrelated to prior jobs, no one cares that you mowed lawns or bussed tables. Describe the skills you learned that can be used to do the job you are applying for, such as communication and leadership skills. A good example could be explaining how you dealt with customers.

- *Feedback.* Have your résumé reviewed by multiple people, such as: a career center staff (if your university has one), a professor or advisor, family and friends, and especially people in your career field. During their career, these people probably wrote numerous résumés for themselves, and there is a chance some revised the résumés of others. They will have much more experience in this area than you, and they can give you feedback assisting you in enhancing your résumé.

- *References.* As part of the application for internships, jobs, and graduate programs, it's very common that applicants be required to present from one to three letters of reference. Sometimes you don't need to present a letter but give the name of a reference that will be contacted by phone or email to talk about you. You will need to build relationships with professors, supervisors, coaches, mentors, and people in your field that can serve as a reference for you when you need it. This type of relationship takes time to build, so you need to think about it in advance. When you request someone to serve as a reference for you, remind them how you met, explain in detail what you are applying for, what they should do (write a letter or talk to someone on the phone) and always send your résumé to assist them with talking about your qualifications.

- *Finding Jobs.* Research shows that most jobs are filled through networking,[197] so we will discuss how to network in detail in the next major section. Larger organizations' websites have a link for "careers"—opportunities and job listings—and you can apply online. Many colleges offer seminars in job-search strategies. Help-wanted ads in newspapers and online job-search services (such as www.indeed.com, www.monster.com, and www.career builder.com) are common places to search for jobs, and www.collegerecruiter. com focuses on internships and entry-level jobs for recent college grads. You can also post your résumé online and create a profile on career-related networking sites, such as **LinkedIn**, and participate in discussion boards to develop online relationships that can lead to a job.

- *When to apply.* When looking to apply for an internship or job, keeping in mind the timeline for the application process is crucial. A lot of organizations post their job vacancies and conduct their searches for a candidate several

EXHIBIT A

Résumé

Will Smith

10 Oak Street
Springfield, MA 01118
(413) 555-3000 / wsmith@aol.com

Objective

Hardworking self-starter seeks sales position at New England Wholesale Foods

Education

Springfield College, Springfield, MA
B.S. Marketing, GPA: 3.4, May 2020

Experience

Big Y Supermarket

100 Cooley St., Springfield, MA 01118, supervisor Fred Fry (413) 782-8273

Marketing Internship Spring Semester 2020

- Helped with the weekly newspaper ad inserts and suggested a layout change that is currently being used
- Worked directly for the store manager on a variety of tasks and projects including Big Data research to better understand customers

Eblens

732 Boston Rd., Springfield, MA 01118, supervisor Julie DeSata (413) 783-0982

Salesperson September to May 2017–2018, 2018-2019

- Sold clothing and footwear to a diverse mix of customers
- July Employee of the Month for having the highest sales volume

Eastern Landscaping

10 Center St., Springfield, MA 01109, supervisor John Fotier (413) 782-7439

Landscaper May 2014–August 2016

- Developed communication skills by interacting with customers and resolving complaints
- Helped get two new customers, which resulted in a 5% increase in sales

Honors and Interests

- Dean's Scholarship: Recipient of academic scholarship for academic achievement excellence
- Basketball: Member of the Springfield College basketball team; captain senior year
- Kappa Delta Pi Honor Society

---

months or even a year in advance. Consider that you will need to have your résumé and cover letter ready, letters of reference in hand, or at least people that agreed to write a recommendation letter for you. You should collect information about the organization you are applying to. Be proactive and start in advance. In addition, if you start early you will not have a problem if you are not called on your first or second application. You will have plenty of time to seek other opportunities. You might gain some experience in the process, and this will give you an advantage as you continue to apply for jobs. You should keep in mind that it's very common to not be successful in the first job application. It might take several tries before you are successful.

- *Employer Information/Research.* In order to prepare for the interview, you should research the organization you have applied to. You want to learn as much about the organization as you can, being able to identify at a minimum the products and/or services it offers, the industry they belong to and its trends, profits (annual report) and vision, mission, values and organizational culture. Large organizations will probably present all this information on its website, and small organizations might present at least part of it. It's common for interviewers to ask questions during the interview process, about your knowledge of their organization. In addition, learning about the organization will give you a chance to think about the fit between the organization's values and your own values.

The Interview—Tips

Your résumé and your references can get you an interview, but how you perform during the interview usually determines whether you get the job. During the interview, you need to convince the person that you can do the job and that you are a good fit for the job, department, and organization culture. Here are some tips related to interviewing, and there are more tips in the follow-up section:

- Before the interview, think about the questions you may be asked, and rehearse your answers. Typical questions might explore: why you are interested in the position, your knowledge about the organization, your strengths and/or weaknesses, and your work experience. In addition, some behavioral questions might request you to give examples, such as a time you accomplished a project, dealt with a difficulty customer, or demonstrated leadership. Take a look at the article "How to Answer the 30 Most Common Interview Questions."[198] The article will assist you in preparing for the interview.

- Don't show up more than 10 minutes early, and never arrive late. Respect the interviewer's time and take into consideration that parking, and finding the right building or office, might take some time.

- It is vital to make a very positive first impression, so your attire and appearance should be appropriate for the job.

- Everyone might be evaluating you including the receptionist, so be polite to everyone you might come in contact with.

- Shut off your phone and never use it during the interview.

- Offer a firm handshake and make direct contact, and use eye contact throughout the interview.

- Bring a copy of your résumé with you; you might want to refer to it during the interview. Sometimes people are nervous and can't remember the name of a former employer or in exactly which period they were interns. Also, bring a notebook to make note of long questions, or of information you learn during the interview.

- Prepare at least three questions about the organization or the job you are applying for that you can ask the interviewee. There is a good chance that by the end of the interview they will ask you what questions you have for them. This will give you an opportunity to demonstrate how much you are interested in the job and the organization, and how much you thought about the fit of the position for you. This is the moment you can stand out from other candidates, since it is likely the other questions may be the same for everyone. This is another reason researching the organization before the interview is crucial.

- Answer the questions directly with details but without long-winded, useless information.

- Your best bet is to wait until you're offered the job before talking about compensation. And you should have done your research to know what the salary range is, because interviewers may ask you how much you expect. But you can try to avoid making the first offer by asking them what the salary range is or what the company has budgeted for the position.

- After the interview, evaluate your own performance; make some notes on what you did and did not do well.

- Send a thank-you card or at least an email to the interviewer, adding anything you forgot to say, stating your interest and the most important reasons you should get the job, and closing by saying that you look forward to hearing from the interviewer. Enclose/attach a copy of your résumé.

- Wait at least a week before checking on your candidacy, because the firm may need to interview more candidates, and it takes time to do a background and reference check. A good method is to ask the interviewer when you can expect to find out if you will be offered the job, and wait until a day after that to follow up.

- Only call the person at the office, and leave a message if you get voice mail.

- If you know that you did not get the job, ask the interviewer for feedback, in order for you to get prepared for future opportunities. You may or may not be told, but an honest answer can be helpful in preparation for future interviews.

Career Services

Many college career-planning services offer workshops on job searching, résumé writing, and how to interview for a job. Some provide the chance to go through a mock interview that is videotaped so you can evaluate yourself afterward. If your career-planning office offers this service, take advantage of it, because you have to nail the interview. It's also very common for city libraries to offer workshops or other resources for job searching and job application. Make sure you ask at your local city library about it.

WORK APPLICATION A-2

Which specific ideas on getting a job do you plan to use?

Helpful Websites

At **MyPerfectResume** (www.myperfectresume.com) you can create a résumé and cover letter and get tips to improve your interview and job searching skills.[199] College students and recent grads can use **College Recruiter** (www.CollegeRecruiter.com) to find internships, entry-level jobs, and careers.[200] **Career Rookie** (www.CareerRookie.com) provides internships, part-time jobs, and entry level careers.[201] You can search for all kinds of jobs, from internships to more experienced jobs on www.indeed.com, www.monster.com, www.career builder.com, and others. In general, these websites have advanced search tools such as choosing a location or region for the job search. If you want to work for a specific organization, go to its website and find the link with titles like "career opportunities."

NETWORKING

>> **LO A-2:** Identify the five steps in the networking process.

>> **LO A-3:** Describe a one-minute self-sell and its three parts.

Networking *is the process of building relationships for the purpose of career building and socializing.* We'll begin by discussing the importance of networking, and then we'll outline the five steps of the networking process.[202]

networking The process of developing relationships for the purpose of career building and socializing.

The Importance of Networking

Networking is the development of relationships with other people that share common interests, by exchanging information and ideas. Networking allows someone to create a pool of people that can serve as a resource for different professional needs such as referring you to someone that is recruiting for a job or writing a letter of reference for you. You have most likely heard the statement "It's not what you know; it's who you know that's important." Networking can result in a more successful job search than mass sending of résumés that often don't lead you to a job interview. If you are referred to someone, they will pay more attention to your résumé than they usually would do for someone that has not been referred to them. A lot of times you know a person that knows someone that is hiring, and they can introduce or refer you to this person, giving you a chance to "get your foot in the door." You will still need to have the qualifications for the job, but being recommended by a familiar person will increase your chances to be invited for an interview.

In addition to getting a job, there are other reasons, you should engage in networking activities:

- To develop personal and professional relationships that might assist you with job mobility.
- To advance within an organization.
- To learn how to perform better at your job.
- To learn how to stay current in your field.
- To get advice and resources to advance your career goals.

Personality Characteristics and Networking

The field of psychology identifies people as having an extrovert or introvert personality type. *Extroverts* are known as people that focus their energy towards other people and feel energized by meeting and talking to new people. On the other side, *introverts* are people that focus their energy inwards, and prefer to do more solitary and reflective activities. Considering that networking implies introducing yourself and maintaining relationships with people you never met before, extroverts often more easily engage in networking activities than introverts. However, both types of personalities may encounter challenges when networking.

An extrovert might easily talk about themselves and forget to show interest in the other person, coming across as a very strong personality, jeopardizing the development of a relationship with others. In that case, asking open-ended questions and putting effort into listening to others might help the extrovert to be more successful in networking situations.

For introverts, it's important to recognize conducting network activities can positively impact their career. Once they recognize its importance they should prepare in advance what they want to say when introducing themselves (we discuss this later in this chapter about the self-sell) and challenge themselves to attend networking events even though this might take them out of their comfort zone. One strategy for introverts could be to invite a colleague to come along with them on network event opportunities. That allows you to walk in the room with someone familiar, and you can introduce yourself to new people with a friend. Once you do this a couple of times, you may feel less stressed in an unfamiliar environment and start to participate in networking events by yourself.

One recommendation is to complete a personality test and verify what type of personality you are. Once you know if you are extrovert or introvert you can use the strategies mentioned above to be more successful in networking. Knowing your personality tendency gives you the power of knowing your strengths and weaknesses and allows you to use it to your own benefit.

When you are looking for a job, get the word out. Tell everyone you know you are looking for work—in person, by phone, and online. Talk to your colleagues, professors, neighbors, leaders in any type of institution or group you belong to. You should let people know what type of job opportunity you are looking for and market yourself to them. Talk with them about your qualifications and experiences, and check if they have anyone they could recommend you contact. After talking with people you know, you will need to start to engage in networking with people you don't know yet.

The five networking steps presented in the sequence will help you to learn how to engage in networking activities. Although a similar networking process is used for both job searches and broad career development, the networking steps presented will focus more on the job search. In the example used, you will be introducing yourself to an expert or senior person in one field that you never met before. This is one of the most common situations in conducting networking, and the beginning of the process of increasing the number of professionals you know in one area and can refer to when needed.

The Networking Process

When you need some help, whom do you turn to? A lot of people will turn to someone from their network. How can you develop a group of different people you can count on? Networking might be the answer. Although, networking sounds easy, and people tend to think that it should come naturally, the reality is that networking is a learned skill that just about everyone struggles with at one time or another. The more you practice the better you get.

Step 1. Perform a Self-Assessment and Set Objectives

Based on your self-assessment in networking, you set narrower objectives. For example, your own networking objectives might include "get a mentor," "determine the expertise, skills, and requirements needed for [a specific job]," and "get feedback on my résumé and job and/or career preparation so that I can be ready to move into [a specific job]."

WORK APPLICATION A-3

Write a networking objective.

Step 2. Create Your One-Minute Self-Sell

Create a brief statement about yourself to help you accomplish your goal. A **one-minute self-sell** *is an opening statement used in networking opportunities that quickly summarizes your history and career plan and asks a question.* Your message must be concise, but it also needs to be clear and compelling, and should not take more than 60 seconds. It should give the listener a sense of your background, identify your career field and a key result you've achieved, and tells the listener what you plan to do next and why. It also should stimulate conversation.

- *History.* Start with a summary of the highlights of your career to date. Briefly describe the internships or jobs you've held and any relevant courses, certification, and other qualifications you have. If you don't have any previous job experience focus on your educational accomplishments.

- *Plans.* Identify the career you are seeking, the industry you prefer, and a specific function or role. You can also mention names of organizations you are targeting and state why you are looking for work.

- *Question.* Finally, ask a question to encourage two-way communication. The question will vary, depending on the person you are networking with and the goal of your one-minute self-sell. For example, you might ask one of the following questions:

  "What areas might offer opportunities for a person with my experience?" "In what other fields can I use these skills or this degree?" "Are there other positions in your organization where my skills could be used?" "What do you think of my career goals? Are they realistic, given my education and skills?" "Do you know of any job openings in my field?"

In your one-minute self-sell, be sure to clearly separate your history, your plans, and your question, and customize your question based on the contact you are talking to. Consider the following example:

one-minute self-sell An opening statement used in networking that quickly summarizes your history and career plan and asks a question.

Hello. My name is Will Smith. I am a senior at Springfield College, graduating in May with a major in marketing, and I have completed an internship in the marketing department at the Big Y supermarket. I'm seeking a job in sales in the food industry. Can you give me some ideas of the types of sales positions available in the food industry?

You also need to remember when in a networking setting, you can't just talk about yourself and your needs. You should also learn about the person you are speaking with. To build a relationship with someone you need to demonstrate genuine interest in learning about the other person and what they do. As the conversation progresses, include questions about the other person too. This will also assist you in mapping what this person could help you with in the future.

Practice delivering your self-sell to family members and friends, and get feedback from them to improve it. The more opportunities you find to use this brief introduction, the easier it becomes. Skill Builder A-3 will give you the opportunity to practice your one-minute self-sell.

WORK APPLICATION A-4

Write a one-minute self-sell to achieve the networking objective you wrote for Work Application A–3.

Step 3. List Your Potential Network Contacts

You should build a network before you need it, so start today. Chances are you have already been involved in networking with **Facebook** or other websites (and don't forget to develop a profile at **LinkedIn** and/or another professional website), so use it along with other networking methods to get a job. Begin with people you know, your primary contacts; look through your email contact address book. It is a good idea to set up a separate email account for professional networking.

Your goal is to create a list of professional and personal contacts. Professional contacts include colleagues (past and present); members of trade or professional organizations and alumni associations; vendors, suppliers, or managers from current or past jobs; and professors, advisors, and mentors. On a personal level, your network includes relatives, neighbors, friends, and even personal service providers (your doctor, dentist, insurance agent, stock broker, accountant, or hairstylist).

Ask your primary contacts for secondary contacts you can network with. You'll want to continually update and add to your list as you get referrals from others. You will discover that your network grows exponentially.

Next, expand your list to include people you don't know. How do you do this? Make a point to go where people gather: fairs and other events in your college and your university that involves internal as well as external stakeholders, meetings of the chamber of commerce, college alumni clubs, college reunions, trade shows, conferences, and career fairs. There are e-groups and chat rooms for all types of interests; seek these out and participate. Get more involved with professional associations; many have special student memberships, and some even have college chapters. To develop your career reputation, become a leader, not just a member, in whatever civic/social/religious organizations you join. Volunteer to be on committees or boards, to give presentations, and so on. When you give a speech, you are instantly networking with everyone in the audience.

Step 4. Conduct Networking Interviews

Consult your list of potential network contacts and set up a networking interview to begin meeting your objective. It may take many interviews to meet a goal, such as getting a job. You may have to begin with an informational interview—a phone call or (preferably) a meeting that you initiate to gain information from a contact who has hands-on experience in your field of interest. In such a situation (in contrast to a job interview), you are the interviewer, so you need to be prepared with specific questions to ask the contact regarding your targeted career or industry.

You'll find that if you ask, many people will agree to talk to you for 15 or 20 minutes. These meetings can be most helpful, especially if you can talk to someone within an organization you'd like to join or in an industry you are targeting. Leave a business card and résumé so the person can contact you in case something comes up. During the interview, be sure to do the following:

- Establish rapport—thank the person for talking with you.

- Deliver your one-minute self-sell, even if the interviewer already heard it.

- Ask your prepared questions, such as "What do you think of my qualifications for this field?" "With your knowledge of the industry, what career opportunities do you see in the future?" "What advice do you have for me as I begin my career?"

- Get additional contacts for your network. You might ask a question like "If you were exploring this field, who else would you talk with?" Most people can give you three names; if you are offered only one, ask for others. Add the new contacts to your network list and plan to interview them. (When contacting new people, be sure to mention who referred you to them.)

- Ask your contact how you might help him or her.

Follow up the interview with a thank-you note and a status report, and enclose your résumé; a handwritten personal note is best, but email can also work for less relevant contacts.

Step 5. Maintain Your Network

It is important to keep members of your network informed of your career progress. Saying "thank you" to those who helped you along the way will strengthen your business relationships; providing updated information about yourself will increase the likelihood of getting help in the future. It is also a good idea to notify everyone in your network that you are in a new position and to provide contact information. Networking doesn't stop once you've made a career change. Make a personal commitment to continue networking in order to be in charge of your career development. Go to trade shows and conventions, make business contacts, and continue to update, correct, and add people to your network list. There is computer software that can help you manage your networking.

Networking is not only about getting help; it's also about helping others, especially those in your network. You will be amazed at how helping others can help you. Try to contact everyone on your network list at least once a year and find out what you can do for him or her. Send congratulations on recent achievements.

Reid Hoffman, founder of **LinkedIn**, is the guru of networking, and he is in constant contact with his network he calls his tribe. He wrote the book on networking, with **Ben Casnocha**, *The Start-Up of You* (Crown, 2012), and there are great excerpts in "The Real Way to Network" and "Three Degrees of Reid Hoffman"; both articles are in *Fortune* (February 6, 2012, pp. 23–32).

APPENDIX SUMMARY

A-1.   List the five steps in career planning.

The steps in the career planning model are (1) completing a self-assessment, (2) determining your career preferences, (3) setting objectives, (4) developing a plan, and (5) controlling the plan.

A-2.   Identify the five steps in the networking process.

The steps in the networking process are (1) performing a self-assessment and setting objectives, (2) creating a one-minute self-sell, (3) developing a list of potential network contacts, (4) conducting networking interviews, and (5) maintaining the network.

A-3.   **Describe a one-minute self-sell and its three parts.**

A one-minute self-sell is an opening statement used in networking that quickly summarizes (1) a person's history and (2) career plan and (3) asks a question to start a conversation.

REVIEW

Key Terms

career development, 349   networking, 355

career planning, 349   one-minute self-sell, 357

Key Term Review

Complete each of the following statements using one of this appendix's key terms.

1. _____ is the process of setting career objectives and determining how to accomplish them.
2. _____ is the process of gaining skill, experience, and education to achieve career objectives.
3. _____ is the process of building relationships for the purpose of career building and socializing.
4. The _____ is an opening statement used in networking that quickly summarizes your history and career plan and asks a question.

SKILL BUILDER A-1

Career Planning

Objective

To develop a career plan.

Skills

The primary skills developed through this exercise are:

1. *Management skill*—decision making (developing career plans)
2. *AACSB competency*—reflective thinking (as you take charge of your career)
3. *Management function*—planning

Preparing for Skill Builder A-1

Answering the following questions will help you develop a career plan. Use additional paper if needed. If your instructor asks you to do this exercise in class, do not reveal anything about yourself that you prefer not to share with classmates.

Step 1. Self-Assessment

A. Write two or three statements that answer the question, "Who am I?" Complete the following personality test: http://www .16personalities.com/free-personality-test. Reflect about your personality characteristics, and how they can give you insights about your career path.

B. Write about two or three of your major accomplishments. (They can be in school, work, sports, or hobbies.) List the skills it took to accomplish each one.

C. Identify skills and abilities you already possess that you can use in your career (for example, skills related to planning, organizing, communicating, or leading).

Step 2. Career Preferences

A. What type of industry would you like to work in? (List as many as interest you.)

B. What type and size of organization do you want to work for?

C. List in priority order, beginning with the most important, the five factors that will most influence your job/career decisions (examples are opportunity for advancement, challenge, security, salary, hours, location of job, travel involved, educational opportunities, recognition, prestige, environment, coworkers, boss, responsibility, and variety of tasks).

D. Describe the perfect job.

E. What type of job(s) do you want during your career (marketing, finance, operations, personnel, and so forth)? After selecting a field, select a specific job (for example, salesperson, manager, or accountant).

Step 3. Career Objectives

A. What are your short-term objectives for the first year after graduation?

B. What are your intermediate-term objectives (the second through fifth years after graduation)?

C. What are your long-range objectives?

D. Make a detailed list of your career goals for the next five to 10 years, identifying the steps to achieving them.

Step 4. Complete an Individual Development Plan

Having reflected in general terms about your career vision, you now have conditions to establish specific goals that can assist you in achieving your vision. These goals must be milestones in your life expressing wishes and positions you seek for yourself and want to strive to achieve them. Establish at least three goals. Your goals should be:

- Clearly formulated
- Easily verifiable over time
- Realistic but challenging
- Worthwhile

After that, describe how you intend to achieve your goals by identifying an action plan. For each defined goal, set deadlines, resources, and activities necessary to accomplish them. This will enable the implementation of your plan.

Goal number 1: Action Plan:

_____

Goal number 2: Action Plan:

_____

Goal number 3: Action Plan:

_____

Step 5. Conduct a Forcefield Analysis

When analyzing your current stage of career and future ambitions, you can see that there are forces that do not necessarily act in the same direction; some are hindering your desired career progression and others are driving forces (see Chapter 6, Exhibit 6-8). These forces can boost or limit your chances of achieving a particular goal of your IDP. Therefore, we are proposing a reflection on the forces that affect your IDP goals to assist you to manage them favorably.

Identify and list the forces or factors that may be favorable (strengths) or unfavorable (weaknesses) to the achievement of your IDP goals, and what you can do to deal with it.

GOALS	FAVORABLE FORCES/STRENGTHS	HOW TO MAXIMIZE THEM
1.		
2.		
3.		

(Continued)

(Continued)

GOALS	UNFAVORABLE FORCES / WEAKNESSES	HOW TO MINIMIZE THEM
1.		
2.		
3.		

Source: This exercise was developed by Erica Berte, associate professor of management, College of Management, Metropolitan State University, Saint Paul, Minnesota.

SKILL BUILDER A-2

Résumé

Objective

To develop a résumé.

Skills

The primary skills developed through this exercise are:

1. *Management skill*—interpersonal (as you communicate your job qualifications)

2. *AACSB competency*—reflective thinking skills (as you take charge of your career), communication (of your qualifications)

3. *Management function*—leading (communication)

Preparing for Skill Builder A-2

Now that you have a career plan, create a résumé that reflects your plan. For help, visit your college career center (if your university offers one) and/or a résumé-building website such as www.resume.com or www.livecareer.com/resume-builder.

Before finalizing your résumé, improve it by using the following assessment procedure.

Résumé Assessment

1. Could a reader understand, within 10 seconds, what job you are applying for and that you are qualified for the position on the basis of skills, experience, and/or education?

2. Does the résumé include an objective that clearly states the position being applied for (such as sales rep)?

3. Does the résumé list skills or experience that support the claim that you can do the job? (For example, if you don't have sales experience, does the résumé list skills developed on other jobs, such as communication skills? Or does it indicate that you have product knowledge or point out that you enjoy meeting new people and that you are able to easily converse with people you don't know?)

4. If education is a major qualification for the job, does the résumé list courses you've taken that prepared you for the position applied for?

5. Does the résumé clearly list your accomplishments and contributions you made during your job experiences to date?

SKILL BUILDER A-3

Networking Skills

Objective

To develop your networking skills.

Skills

The primary skills developed through this exercise are:

1. *Management skill*—interpersonal (as you communicate your job qualifications)

2. *AACSB competency*—reflective thinking skills (as you take charge of your career), communication (of your qualifications)

3. *Management function*—leading (communication)

Preparing for Skill Builder A-3

Review the appendix section on the networking process, and complete the following steps.

1. Perform a self-assessment and set objectives. List two or three of your accomplishments, and set an objective—for example, to learn more about career opportunities in your major or to get an internship or a part-time, summer, or full-time job.

2. Practice the one-minute self-sell that you wrote for Work Application A-4.

3. Develop your network. List at least five people to be included in your network, preferably individuals who can help you achieve your objective.

4. Conduct a networking interview. To help meet your objective, select one person from your network list to interview (by phone if it is not possible to meet in person) for about 20 minutes. Write questions to ask during the interview.

Source: This exercise was developed by Andra Gumbus, associate professor, College of Business, Sacred Heart University. © Andra Gumbus, 2002. It is used with Dr. Gumbus's permission.

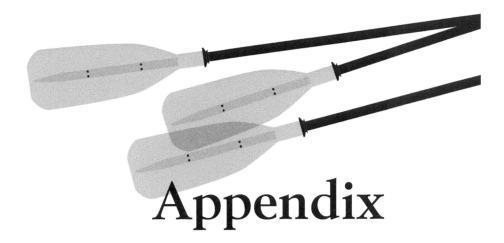

Appendix

Guide to Student Team Projects

One of the best ways to teach teamwork skills is in the context of a large-scale team project that requires team problem solving (Goltz, Hietapelto, Reinsch, & Tyrell, 2008). An unstructured real-world problem can be used as a mechanism for teaching both teamwork and problem-solving skills. The team assignment needs to be challenging and motivating (Rentz, Arduser, Meloncon, & Debs, 2009). When designing team projects, it is important to consider problem design (What are the characteristics of the task?), team design (How do students get chosen for the team?), process design (How do students manage the team process?), and evaluation design (How is student input included in the evaluation?).

Many times, students are assigned team projects with limited preparation or training about how to work in teams (Snyder, 2009). If professors do not provide instruction on how to work in teams, they should not be surprised by poor team performance and dissatisfied students. Student team members need help to deal with the following challenges: understanding the purpose of the project, encouraging participation among team members, planning the project, keeping a project on track, and negotiating conflicts. All these topics are discussed in this book.

This appendix contains advice and tools to help students conduct a team project and learn from the experience. Although there are a lot of activities at the beginning of the project, student teams that spend time planning for teamwork and taskwork are more successful in the long run (Mathieu & Rapp, 2009). The following sections present guidelines on starting the team, planning and developing the project, monitoring the project and maintaining teamwork, performing team writing, and wrapping up and completing the

369

project. It is up to the students to work through this structure and manage their group process in order to successfully complete their team project.

A.1 Starting the Team

Team Warm-Ups

Team warm-ups are social activities designed to help the team members get to know each other. Forming social relations at the beginning of a team project helps build trust and improve communications throughout the project. Building social relations is something teams should do at the very beginning, from the first team meeting. Once the team project gets going, team members don't want to spend time building social relations—they want to focus on the task. So, for the first three weeks of your team project, start your team meetings with a 10-minute warm-up activity (see Figure A.1).

These activities encourage self-disclosure—telling the other team members about yourself. However, this is a limited self-disclosure suitable for a work environment. You have a right to privacy, so be open with your teammates, but do not feel obliged to share more than would be appropriate to share in a work environment.

Development of a Team Contract

An important part of starting a team is to obtain agreement about the purpose or goals of the team, the roles and responsibilities of the team members, norms or operating rules, and expectations about the performance of team members. The contract provides an initial commitment and direction for the team about how members will work together. It focuses on the teamwork process rather than on the task aspects of the team project.

When thinking about team goals, try to develop three to five goals. The goals can be about the task, the group process, or what members hope to accomplish working on the project. For example, is your focus getting a good grade, learning a lot about teamwork, or getting along with the other students? It is better to write specific goals rather than general goals. Objectives are the specific actions or criteria that relate to your goals. Objectives should be written so that they are measurable and the team can evaluate whether the goals were met.

Team members should discuss what they expect from each other. What are the primary roles and responsibilities of team members? This includes

Figure A.1   Team Warm-Ups

Week 1 Team Warm-Up

Each member should introduce herself or himself to the team, in turn. Have each tell name, major, hometown, and other biographic information.

Discuss the following topics by taking turns answering these questions:

- What is your favorite movie? Why?
- What was your favorite class or instructor? Why?
- What do you like most and least about team projects?

Week 2 Team Warm-Up

Have the group members discuss several of the following questions:

- What is one of your favorite jokes?
- Describe your favorite vacation, recreation activity, or sport.
- What is your favorite music? List the top three songs you listen to now.
  (Research shows college students are good at assessing personality from music.)

Have group members discuss these topics about working on team projects:

- What types of work do you like best? What types of work do you like least?
  (This may help you assign roles later in the project.)

Week 3 Team Warm-Up

- Have each team member privately write down three names that would be good for the team.
- List all the team members' ideas.
- Have the team create a new list that does not include any names already listed.
- Try to select a name for your team that is supported by all members.
- If there is time, develop a team logo to go with the name.

SOURCE: Adapted from Scholtes, P. (1988). *The team handbook: How to use teams to improve quality.* Madison, WI: Joiner.

both task and relationship issues. Does the team expect equal commitment and participation from each member? How important is it that assignments are done on time or that work is high quality? How important is working cooperatively and maintaining good social relations? What is important to you as a team member? Try to be specific about these expectations.

Meeting rules or team norms define the appropriate behaviors for the team and its members. There are a variety of issues to consider when establishing norms. How should decisions be made? What are legitimate reasons for missing meetings? What should be done when people miss too many meetings? How important is it that everyone participates in team discussions? When assignments are made, what should be done when team members do not complete them? Who is responsible for the agenda and minutes? How should conflicts and disagreements be handled? How can the team encourage members to listen attentively and respectfully to others? What should the team do to enforce its rules?

One of the main complaints people have about their performance evaluations is that they did not know what was expected of them. You have just discussed the roles and responsibilities of team members and the operating rules for the team. Should these expectations be included in team members' performance evaluations? What criteria should be used to evaluate each team member's performance?

To develop a team contract, team members should think about the team's goals, objectives, roles, norms, and performance expectations. Then, the team should come to an agreement on these topics to create a written team charter. Figure A.2 presents a format for the development of a team contract.

Figure A.2   Team Contract

---

a. *Team Goals:* What are the main goals of your team?

b. *Team Objectives:* What specific actions or criteria relate to these goals? How can these be measured or evaluated?

c. *Team Member Roles:* What are the primary roles and responsibilities of each team member?

d. *Team Norms:* What operating rules does the team need?

e. *Team Member Evaluation:* What criteria will be used to evaluate each member's performance?

SOURCE: Adapted from Herrenkohl, R. (2004). *Becoming a team*. Mason, OH: South-Western.

Leadership and Meeting Roles

Teams often establish meeting roles to help meetings operate more efficiently. The two most common meeting roles are team leader and recorder. The team leader has two functions: set up the agenda and facilitate the team meeting. The team's agenda is designed to structure the meeting and is related to the tasks the team is performing. The leader acts as a facilitator who ensures that information is shared and processed by the team in a supportive and participative environment. This includes keeping the team discussion on track, preventing personal criticism, and ensuring participation by all team members. The team recorder takes notes on key decisions and task assignments in order to provide documentation of the team's activities.

Student teams usually make the mistake of selecting a team leader at the first meeting. Unfortunately, they often pick the most talkative person rather than the person best suited for structuring the team's task or facilitating team meetings. During the first three weeks of a team project, the leader role should be rotated. After that, the team can decide to keep rotating or select a permanent leader. Use the Team Role Analysis (Figure A.3) to help make your decision.

Managing Team Technology

Regardless of whether team members are collocated or are scattered around the world, project teams rely on technology for communication and managing project documents. Even when teams regularly meet face-to-face, they often use technology for both task and social communication.

Successful use of technology by teams requires addressing several issues. First, all team members need to agree on which technologies to use for various functions. Second, the team needs to make sure that everyone has sufficient capacity to use the technologies. This means that all team members have the technologies available to them and they have the skills to use the technologies. Finally, there needs to be agreement about the norms for use of the selected technology.

There are a variety of norms that teams may decide to develop about the use of technology. Here are some of the questions teams should discuss when developing technology norms. Which technology should be used for different types of communication? What is the appropriate length and response time for different technologies (for example, email versus texting)? When should messages or replies be sent to everyone on the team? What are the rules for modifying or editing shared documents? When does an issue, decision, or conflict require a face-to-face meeting?

Figure A.3   Team Role Analysis

For the past three weeks, your team has been rotating the roles of leader and recorder. It is now time to decide how to handle these role issues in the future.

Step 1: Analyze your team's leadership.

Each team member should anonymously write down who has emerged as the informal leader of the team. Compare and discuss the answers:

- Do the team members agree on who is the leader?
- How did someone become the leader or why did a team leader not emerge?

Step 2: How should team leadership operate in the future?

- Should someone be appointed the team's leader?
- Should the role of leader continue to be rotated at each meeting?
- Who should be the leader?

Step 3: Which of the following activities define the team leader's role?

_____ The leader facilitates the team meetings.

_____ The leader coordinates and/or directs the team project.

_____ The leader is the editor of the team project.

_____ Other leader roles _____

Step 4: What other roles should the team have?

- Does the team need a recorder and other meeting roles?
- Who should fulfill these roles?

As a team, complete the Team Project Technology Survey (Figure A.4) in order to develop agreement about your team's use of technology and to identify potential technology problems.

A.2 Planning and Developing the Project

Challenge the Assignment

When given an assignment, most teams jump right in and start to solve what they view as the problem. Often, they work on their initial ideas until it is obvious that their first approach is not working, at which point they go

Figure A.4   Team Project Technology Survey

List the technology and software your team selected to

    communicate task-related information _____

    communicate social-related information _____

    manage your project documents _____

How effective are these technologies at performing the listed functions?

(rate from 1—not at all effective, 2—somewhat effective, 3—effective, 4—very effective)

    _____ Communicate task-related information

    _____ Communicate social-related information

    _____ Manage your project documents

What are the benefits of using technology in your team project?

_____

What problems have you encountered using technology?

_____

Develop norms about the use of technology for your team.

_____

back to the beginning and start over. This is a very inefficient and frustrating approach.

Take time at the beginning to understand the assignment. Ask your professor questions about the assignment. Develop an overall plan and then question whether it will work. At the second and third team meetings, review the project assignment and the direction your team is taking. Ask the following questions: What are the benefits of our approach to the assignment? What are the problems with our approach to the assignment? Should we change our approach? It is better to change direction earlier rather than later in the project.

Generation of Project Ideas

Student project teams often face their most difficult decision at the beginning—selecting a project topic or initial direction. If the team is having trouble developing and agreeing to ideas, try using some team creativity techniques. The following is a modified brainwriting approach that is useful.

Brainwriting Method

1. *Write.* Have each team member write down at least five ideas.

2. *Review.* Combine all the ideas into a large list (or use sticky notes and cover a wall). Review the list and combine or link ideas that are related.

3. *Multivote.* Allow each team member to select three alternatives he or she would like to support. Tally the votes and remove items that received no votes or only one vote. Discuss the alternatives that have been selected, and look for new ways to combine or synthesize alternatives. If necessary, repeat this process until there are five or fewer ideas.

4. *Decide.* Use consensus decision making to select an alternative. Avoid arguing for your own position without listening to the position of others. Do not try to reach a quick agreement by voting or tossing a coin. Try to get others to explain their position so that you better understand the differences. Look for creative and collaborative solutions, such as integrating alternatives.

Project Planning

Planning is an ongoing activity for a team. To plan a project, the team needs to break the project down into its basic parts, develop a schedule proposing length of time to perform the parts and the necessary sequence to complete the parts, and assign team members to work on the parts. A project timeline is a simple graphical representation of a team project. Figure A.5 shows a project timeline for a 10-week student research project. You should try to develop a project timeline for your team project and consult it regularly to track your progress. It is useful to include some milestone reviews—times when you will review the team's progress and modify the project plan if needed.

Roles and Assignments

Although we call it teamwork, individuals working alone who use team meetings to coordinate their activities often do most of the work on a team project. Consequently, dividing a project into various tasks, assigning individuals to perform tasks, and monitoring the completion of tasks are important team functions.

Team projects can be divided in a number of ways. The overall project can be divided into report sections (Introduction, Analysis, Discussion), or activities (data gathering, analysis, writing). Individuals can be assigned certain tasks, while the team as a whole may perform other tasks. Team members need to negotiate these role assignments with each other. Remember, equity is less a matter of whether everyone is doing the same amount of

Figure A.5   Project Timeline

Project Activity	Responsible Persons	Weeks									
		1	2	3	4	5	6	7	8	9	10
Develop goals and team contract		■									
Select a project topic			■	■							
Collect research articles			■	■							
Write literature review					■		■	■	■		
Develop research methods					■						
Gather research data						■	■				
Analyze data and create tables							■	■			
Write research results								■	■		
Write project paper									■	■	
Edit paper									■		
Develop presentation										■	■
Conduct presentation											■
Review project at milestones						■			■		

work, and more about whether everyone is pulling his or her own weight and is equally invested in the outcome.

The most common approach used by student teams is to divide the project and assign one person to perform each part. Team meetings are used to monitor progress and coordinate activities. A few parts of the project (making strategic decisions or reviewing the final report) are left to the team as a whole. This is an efficient approach, but it leaves the team vulnerable to a team member who fails to perform his or her role. An alternative approach is the pair system, where at least two people are assigned to each major activity, and everyone works on more than one part of the project. This approach encourages coordination and integration and protects the team from problem team members.

To create roles and assignments, the team needs to discuss the following issues:

Which parts of the project should be divided and assigned to individuals?

Which parts of the project should be done by all team members?

Who should be assigned to work on various parts of the project?

Should there be a project leader to coordinate activities?

Should the team have an editor who is responsible for putting together the final report?

The team should develop an action plan that lists the major team assignments, who is responsible for performing them, and what results are expected. The action plan needs to be periodically reviewed and modified during the course of the project.

Reevaluation of the Project and Approach

Is this a good project topic? How can we improve or refine our definition of the project? Is our approach a good one? Are we headed in the right direction? These are very good questions to ask about the team's initial project decisions. These are even better questions to ask during the second week of a project rather than during a midpoint crisis. Try completing a Force Field Analysis (Figure A.6) to assist the team with these questions and answers.

A Force Field Analysis starts when you list the driving and restraining forces related to your project topic or approach. After you list these forces, highlight the most important ones. Next, review your project by discussing the following issues:

Is this a good project topic or approach? Should we accept it or reject it?

How can we improve or refine our approach?

What additional information do we need to develop our approach to the project?

Figure A.6   Force Field Analysis: Are We Going in a Good Direction?

Driving Forces	Restraining Forces
Factors that make this a good project (i.e., what are the benefits of this project topic or approach?)	Factors that limit the success of this project (i.e., what are the problems with this project topic or approach?)

A.3 Monitoring the Project and Maintaining Teamwork

Team Meetings: Sharing Information, Making Decisions, and Tracking Assignments

Team meetings are used to coordinate activities, track progress, make decisions, and assign tasks. Team meetings should start with sharing information and reviewing progress. Team members check in by updating the team on their activities and work assignments. If the team has developed a project plan and timeline, it can review its progress on meeting the objectives. After reviewing progress, team meetings then focus on decision making. Decisions relate to project topics, management of the team, team activities, task assignments, and coordination of tasks. At the end of the meeting, important decisions are summarized and task assignments reviewed.

Teams need to plan their project by outlining the various tasks, deciding when the tasks need to be completed, and assigning team members to perform the tasks. Once the planning has been completed, the team should regularly review its progress on meeting these objectives. The Weekly Action Plan (Figure A.7) is a good way to record assignments at the end of a team meeting. It also makes a good starting point for reviewing performance at the next meeting.

It is the team leader's job to help structure and facilitate the team meeting. Simple agendas that outline the meeting structure (information sharing, progress check, team decisions, and task assignments) and identify decision topics are useful to keep the team on track. The leader can ask for input on

Figure A.7   Weekly Action Plan

Action	Responsible Person	Expected Result	Completion Date

the agenda either before or at the beginning of the meeting. The recorder monitors progress of the meeting and records the major decisions and task assignments.

Group Process Evaluations

Once the team has started working on its project, the team needs to monitor its progress, manage problems, and improve how it is operating. Student teams fall into behavior patterns fairly quickly. They often adopt patterns they used before in other team projects or classroom settings. These behavior patterns become stable ways of operating, even when they are not adaptive or effective. This is why it is important to set aside time to evaluate how the team is operating.

One of the biggest problems for improving teams is to get beyond scapegoating or blaming individuals (or outside forces) for the team's problems. It is not problem people who are causing difficulties—it is a team process that does not work. Your team has to accept responsibility that they allow problem behaviors to occur and continue. Scapegoating never leads to solutions. It is just a way of blaming others for the problem so the team does not have to work on a solution.

The team must decide whether it wants to live with its problems (and problem people) or whether it wants to evaluate what it is doing and develop strategies to work together more effectively. Team members often ignore problems ("don't make waves") until the problems are very disruptive and difficult to solve. It is better to identify problems early and deal with them before they disrupt the team's operation. Regular group process evaluations are one way to do this.

Group process evaluations are performed at the end of team meetings. They help identify what the team is doing right and encourage dealing with team problems. Have each team member rate the team's performance and then answer the following questions: What is the team doing well? What areas of improvement are needed? (See Figure A.8.) After answering these questions, discuss the responses in the team. Use the discussion to acknowledge accomplishments, identify problems, and develop solutions for the team's problems.

Student teams should conduct group process evaluations about every other week. This helps ensure that problems are identified before they become too difficult to manage. It is useful for students to save their evaluations to track the team's progress. The group process evaluation forms are a good history of the team's performance and are useful for evaluating and learning from the team project experience.

Managing Problem Behaviors

Group process evaluations are good at identifying the problems teams encounter, but how should the team manage these problems? This activity is a method that teams can use to manage problem behaviors. The team can try it on a sample problem to learn how the approach works or use it on a problem the team is trying to resolve. Figure A.9 presents a format for this activity.

Figure A.8   Group Process Evaluation

How well is the team performing?								
Very Poorly	1	2	3	4	5	6	7	Very Well
What is the team doing well?								
What areas of improvement are needed?								

Figure A.9   Managing Problem Behaviors Activity

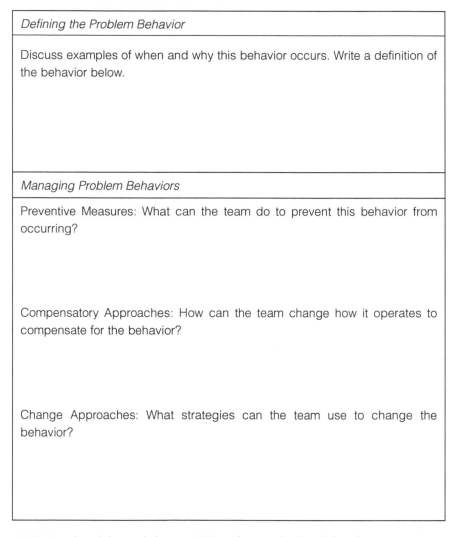

Defining the Problem Behavior

Discuss examples of when and why this behavior occurs. Write a definition of the behavior below.

Managing Problem Behaviors

Preventive Measures: What can the team do to prevent this behavior from occurring?

Compensatory Approaches: How can the team change how it operates to compensate for the behavior?

Change Approaches: What strategies can the team use to change the behavior?

SOURCE: Adapted from Scholtes, P. (1994). *The team handbook for educators.* Madison, WI: Joiner.

The first step is to select and define the problem behavior. There are many behaviors that can disrupt a team's operation. If the team has discussed team norms, then problem behaviors can be viewed as actions that violate these norms. Common problems for teams are poor attendance, failure to complete assignments on time, dominating team discussions, or interpersonal conflicts among team members. The team should select a problem that it wants to handle better in the future.

After selecting a problem behavior for analysis, try to better define the behavior. Think of specific examples of the problem behavior. Discuss when the behavior occurs and what is causing it. What team norms does it violate? Write a definition of the behavior.

There are several approaches to managing problem behaviors. The team can try to prevent the behavior from occurring, it can compensate for the behavior by changing how the team operates, or it can try to use rewards or punishments to change the behavior. For the problem behavior identified, discuss alternative approaches for the team to manage the problem behavior and write your answers.

After completing this analysis, the team is ready to decide how it wants to deal with the problem behavior. Regardless of whether the team decides to do nothing or adopt one of the strategies identified in the activity, the team should review the status of the problem at its next meeting.

Milestone: Midpoint Evaluation

The midpoint of the project cycle is a time when teams often evaluate what they are doing. Although it is halfway through the project's period, most teams discover that the project is less than half completed. What is worse is that the team may doubt whether they are headed in the right direction. It is time to stop and reevaluate the team's goals and objectives, the direction of the project, and the way the team is operating. You might want to go back and review the team's contract, conduct a Force Field analysis on the project's direction, or review and modify the project timeline so it reflects the team's actual performance. Finally, do a group process evaluation and review how well your team is working together.

A basic midpoint evaluation technique for reflecting on the team's performance is the Start-Stop-Continue Approach (Dyer, Dyer, & Dyer, 2007). Individual team members write down what they think the team should start doing, stop doing, and continue doing in order to be more effective. The team discusses these views and looks for patterns or common responses. The team leader asks for concrete examples of the identified issues. Next, the team discusses ways to change what they are doing to become more effective.

After the midpoint, teams need to make a push toward performance. Working hard to complete the project is only useful if you are heading in the right direction and have a group process that supports teamwork. Now is the time as a team to make sure that this happens and the project moves forward.

A.4 Performing Team Writing

Writing in a team is not easy. There are lots of problems that can arise, from personality clashes to computer incompatibilities. There is no definitive approach that is the best way for a team to write together. The success of various approaches depends on the group size and the personalities and abilities of the team members.

Writing in a team is risky. You have to give up control and learn to accept differences in writing styles. You must also deal with writing and decision-making issues at the same time. This is very confusing because you some-times do not know whether the disagreement is about what you said or how you are saying it. Added to these problems is fear—the fear that your grade will be affected and you will not get credit for your good work.

Overall Strategy

Writing a team paper usually has three parts: defining and outlining the project, writing the sections, and reviewing and editing. Students often go too quickly through the first stage and end up with a lot of problems and confusion later on. Students also forget about the third stage, so the final project can have the appearance of being thrown together at the last moment. Recognizing the importance of all three stages makes team writing easier and improves the quality of the project.

When defining the nature of the project, the team should discuss the par-ticular content of the final document, which requires development of an outline of the final report and a team discussion about what information is to be presented. Try to anticipate problems, such as dealing with problem team members and keeping on schedule. Establishing a work plan with assignments and due dates helps manage some of these problems.

The team needs to decide how to divide the writing. The next section presents several options to accomplish this task. However, before you send your team members out to write their sections, you need to establish some ground rules. How long should the sections be? Should people submit drafts or relatively finished text? Should the team review the detailed outlines before writing drafts?

Although the team should develop the project's overall outline collabora-tively, there are many options for dividing up the writing and editing tasks. Although dividing the assignment is efficient (especially since it reduces meeting times), at some point everyone needs to review and edit the docu-ment. You have not done your part if you have not reviewed and agreed with (or offered modifications) to the entire document.

Division of Work

There is no single preferred method to divide up the tasks of writing a report. A team's options range from having one person write the entire report with information provided by team members, to all the team members collaboratively writing the report together. In most cases, teams select an approach between these extremes, where the project is divided and individual team members write sections of the report. Regardless of your selection, there are two additional elements to the divide and write approach: the weak editor system and the strong editor system. Your team should discuss how you want to write the project using these approaches as a starting point for your discussion.

1. *Weak editor:* Divide the paper into sections and assign the writing of parts. This is probably the most common approach to team writing. It makes logical sense because it uses division of labor. However, it often leads to papers that are difficult to read because the sections do not flow smoothly together. Using this approach still requires a good editing system to help deal with the overlaps and missing information that inevitably occurs.

If your team is using this approach, then you need to spend time at the beginning defining what the sections of the paper should look like. Obviously, this includes having a good report outline so the sections do not repeat or overlap. In addition, there need to be rules about how to make the parts as compatible as possible. For example, how should each section end so the next section flows into it smoothly? Some options for writing rules include the size of each section, agreement on the key terms to use throughout the report, typical paragraph length, formatting and layout, and computer compatibility issues.

2. *Strong editor:* In this approach, a central editor controls most of the writing process. Although your team may elect to have individual team members work on separate sections of the report, you may want to take a more centralized approach to writing the final document. For example, the team members submit drafts of their sections of the report to a central editor who finishes the drafts and cobbles the sections together. This approach often leads to a more integrated report, but it puts stress and a lot of responsibility on a key team member.

From the professor's perspective, this is a good approach: The report is easier to read because the writing style is more consistent. However, it does create a few problems for the team. It requires better planning because the drafts of the sections have to be submitted earlier to give time for the editor to put them all together. The editor has to put in extra work, which means that you are using your team's best writer to integrate work rather than to write important sections. Additionally, similar to other centralized approaches, it also creates problems about how to select and reward the team member who takes this central role.

Most student teams select the weak editor approach, where the editor's job is merely to cut and paste parts of the report. This approach is easy for the students, but it can create problems in the paper. Often, student team reports have unexplained gaps between sections or sections that overlap with each other. The terminology used in one part of the report might be different from other parts, as a result the reader is often uncertain if new concepts are really being used. Also, language and writing style differences can make a team paper hard to read. The strong editor approach helps to deal with these writing problems. The main difficulty with the strong editor approach is that it takes time. The parts of the report must be submitted to the editor early enough that the editor can work on the paper and have the team members review the final product. Regardless of which approach a team uses, everyone is responsible for the report. No team member is finished with the assignment until he or she has reviewed the final draft!

The use of technology for team writing allows an alternative approach: reciprocal composition (Duarte & Snyder, 2006). In this approach, an outline of the report is stored in an electronic database that is available to all team members. Team members work on all parts of the report by adding and editing material. Electronic document-writing tools allow the team to monitor each other's participation in the writing process and the changes being made to the report. This approach can be very efficient because it allows all team members to work simultaneously. However, it requires a tightly structured agenda to ensure progress on all parts of the document.

A.5 Wrapping Up and Completing the Project

Milestone: Precompletion Planning

Several weeks before the final project is due, it is time for a review meeting to evaluate the situation and plan for completion of the project. This is similar to the other milestone evaluations (such as the midpoint review), except the focus is on how to complete the project. If all is going well, this evaluation is just reviewing the project plan, coordinating submissions of material to the editor, and arranging a final review meeting. If things are not going as planned, now is the time to decide how to salvage the situation by reassigning tasks, redefining expectations about tasks and activities, or even negotiating a new contract with your professor. Even if you are having problems, your team still has some options in order to finish successfully within the next two weeks.

Team Evaluations

In many student team projects, the professor allows some student input on team member evaluations. This is appropriate, since students know more about the performance of individual team members than the professor. It is time to review the team's contract to see what performance expectations your team decided were relevant. You should use these to evaluate your teammates, since it is not fair to evaluate people on new criteria or to evaluate different team members using different criteria.

Teams have evaluation biases. Teams tend to give everyone high evaluations when the team is successful and to scapegoat or blame a few members when the team performs poorly. Instead, you should try to honestly evaluate your teammates using the criteria your team established. It is fine to give mostly positive evaluations when your team worked well together, but it is not fair to give everyone a high evaluation if that does not reflect individual contributions.

Celebrating Success and Learning From the Experience

Congratulations—you finished your team project. If your team was like most project teams, you had your ups and downs along the way, with challenges and conflicts to manage. Your team should celebrate its success with a social event.

This is not likely to be your last team project as a student or professional, so you should try to learn as much as possible from the experience. If you have been saving your group process evaluations, now is a good time to review them to try to understand the teamwork process. How did your evaluations of the team's performance change during the course of the project? What were the things that your team did well during the project? What were the areas where improvement was needed? Was your team able to resolve its problems along the way?

A final group process evaluation that examines the entire project experience can be a valuable learning tool. Remember that people learn more from positive feedback than they do from negative feedback. Make sure you try to understand what went right about the project so you can repeat it in the future.